Self-Made:
How to Win by Investing in Yourself

Written by:
Carling D. Colbert, Sr.

CP

Cadmus Publishing
www.cadmuspublishing.com

Published by Cadmus Publishing
www.cadmuspublishing.com
Port Angeles, WA

ISBN: 978-1-63751-071-1
Library of Congress Control Number: 2021921382

Cover Artist: L. Caldwell

DEDICATION:

I would like to dedicate my work to my beautiful mother, Betty M. Thomas, who gave me life and loved me despite circumstances. This also goes out to my wonderful children: Carlee A'Tyshia-Bethani Colbert; Carling Durrell Colbert II; Daniel Cyntier Colbert, and Landen Tyler-Alexzander Colbert. I love you all and wrote this as a testament to a better future for our generation and generations to come.

ACKNOWLEDGEMENTS

I would like to first give thanks to the Great Architect of the Universe for the mighty blessing that had been bestowed upon me, and for keeping me in the light when darkness was all around me. Secondly, I want to acknowledge my three lovely sisters for supporting me over the last few years, especially my knee-baby, Ennis D. Thomas-Samuel. I couldn't have done this without you, literally. I also want to thank my friends and associates that I've met through the military, especially those post military who have been support systems. This book has been a blessing to my life and I wouldn't have started the writing process if it wasn't for encouragement from my two college professors, Angela Consoni and Dr. Waller, who both taught at the Community College I attended.

I also want to give thanks to the people who are no longer here that gave me valuable lessons of the world that I've used throughout this publication. And to those of you who purchased this book, I send you my deepest gratitude. Your support will not only help me and my family, but others as well. I've made an obligation to give back by contributing a portion of all sales on any book I publish to *Operation HOT GRITS* and other charities/organizations. You can read more about it in the section about who I am at the end of the book. Finally, I'd like to thank my publisher and everyone who helped bring this to fruition from the artist, to the editors, and all the distributors who now have a place for me on their shelf or e-book catalog. I am thankful that a young Black man from a small town called Reynolds, Georgia can have a big impact on so many people. May the Great Architect of the Universe continue to shine his light on you all. So, mote it be.

Introduction

Were you financially impacted by the COVID-19 pandemic? Did it cost you or someone you know their job? Was the government and those "stimulus" packages a life raft during a chaotic 2020? If you answered "yes" to any of these questions, then you chose the right book to help prevent another financial outbreak. This publication was written with several goals that I seek to accomplish by the time you finish reading it:

- Establish a financial foundation on which you can build
- Expand your knowledge base on various financial investments/securities in which to build wealth and create cash flows
- Educate you on IRA wealth building strategies and
- Extinguish the preconceived notion that money is evil

I know it may not be possible to accomplish the following goals with one or two books, but if I can achieve just one of them with you by the end of your read, then this book is a success.

Success in life is about becoming what you want to be, and by purchasing this book I deduce that you want to change your current financial situation. Therefore, I'd like to thank you for choosing this particular title to begin your journey to becoming self-made. Since a young age, I wanted to be financially free but grew up being taught that money was evil, especially having a lot of it. There were people in my socioeconomic group that didn't truly understand the concept of money and continued to spread this vicious untruth when the truth is the love of money is the root of all evil. It wasn't until I hit rock bottom and had a burning desire to change my financial situation, thus allowing my superior self to shine, that I was able to become a self-made man. Not everyone who has obtained financial success is greedy or unscrupulous. Yes, there are people who have achieved their status in life by using unsavory methods and this, more than likely, stemmed from a scarcity mentality, as well as, a lack of knowledge about money and finance. However, this doesn't describe everyone who has achieved self-made status. To get where I want to take you in this book, it's important to start having an abundance mentality. By thinking in this manner, you'll start to look differently at the world and concepts like money, education, risks, and work.

Money

Money is a construct that was created as a medium of exchange or store of value; it's essentially what we agree it is. Back in the day it was cattle; for some people it's stones; and for others, inmates, it could be based on a bartering system that consists of cigarettes, food, drugs, or some other form of entertainment that serves as currency. The currency that we have in the United States was once based on the gold standard and made it worth something, but was taken off that standard in 1971, when former-President Richard Nixon closed the "gold window." This then put us on the dollar standard, which is a fiat currency. What that means is that the currency is worth whatever the issuing entity states it's worth. It's based on trust and faith that the strength of the currency will last and not become worthless. This is why you need an abundance mentality and the ability to think differently about money. Maybe one day soon there will be no physical currency and it will all be digital. We already have Bitcoin and non-fungible tokens (NFT) that are taking over. Money has changed forms multiple times throughout the years and will continue to evolve; so should you.

A large number of people who are considered poor or middle class tend to see money as a way to get things, while the rich and wealthy see it as a tool to invest. Take how lower income people create scams, some wealthy individuals, too, that take money away from people only to spend it and come up with some new scheme. Or take how when lower income people get raises, bonuses, or a tax refund, most tend to spend it on things of no real value, or their expenses rise with their pay. I may be philosophical when I say this, but if you look closely at my previous statement about money being what we agree it is, then you can essentially get something for nothing. Imagine if you purchased a multifamily apartment complex with today's U.S. Dollar and five years from now the dollar becomes worthless or all currency becomes digital. You seemingly got this building for nothing. Also, for the record, I'm not advocating that you don't enjoy the fruits of you labor and only invest, what I am saying is that most people choose, whether consciously or unconsciously, to buy things out of lack of understanding while others that are more knowledgeable, buy things out of abundance. An abundance mentality will allow you to change your thinking. Take for instance how a multibillionaire lost over a billion dollars in the stock market during a one-day period, and how he made a joke about losing so much money. Some people probably would have gone insane, committed suicide, or felt life was over. That didn't happen with this gentleman because he understood the concepts of money and was able to shrug the loss off because he knew he could make that billion back, and more. I'm sure people complained about what could've been done with so much money, but that's the way life goes. If you look at the bigger picture, then no one can be kept poor because opportunity has been taken away or because certain people monopolized all the wealth. New money is literally printed or created daily, and trillions of dollars change hands in a matter of milliseconds in the markets, so stop focusing on what everyone else has and start focusing on what you want, and you can get. There is enough to go around for everyone and it's not difficult if you stop having a limited mindset.

To become financially successful or self-made, you have to stop thinking of spending and think more on investing and acquiring assets. If not, then you'll continue to stay in the lifecycle of working for money, paying taxes, and hoping that circumstance will change, i.e., you hitting the lottery or receiving a large raise. Once you begin to see money for what it is, a tool to invest, then you can begin to achieve a level of financial freedom that you crave and finally become self-made.

Education

Words can be used interchangeably and can often be subjective. Therefore, I encourage you to have an operational definition for yourself of what financial freedom, success, and being self-made means. I am a believer that it's not possible to live a really complete and successful life unless you have some similitude of financial success or wealth. You can be happy with what you have and live a decent life, but in order to do so you still need money. If that's the case, then why not live life and enjoy it to the fullest? Making money is not difficult in today's time, especially with the advent of the Internet. Instead of browsing social media sites and posting selfies, why not use the world's two most powerful tools, your brain and the internet, to make thousands or even millions. Information is at its most accessible, unlike during my time when you had to go to the library, check-out books. or read newspaper articles and reviews to get information.

Educating yourself on a subject leads to wisdom and wisdom leads to abundance. I can attest to this because I wanted to learn everything I could about finance. I was ignorant on the subject until I start reading and getting the knowledge. My education began with two books: *The Complete Day Trader* and *The Richest Man in Babylon*. Since then, I have continued to expand my knowledge base into trading and investing in instruments such as stocks, dividends, commodities, futures and options, real estate, debt, and other financial systems.

My desire to learn and change my socioeconomic status far outweighed the situation I was in. My top goal has been to create wealth and not be at the mercy of an employer to give me a job. If you want to succeed, then your desire must be stronger than the need to save, hang with family and friends, or living paycheck to paycheck.

Achieving the financial success of self-made status is no different than doing simple math—both require a process that must be followed to achieve an end result. The only difference is that math is a science and becoming self-made is a hybrid of art and science. To get where I'm taking you, it doesn't matter where you come from because anyone can achieve success if they have the ability to think, understand and apply key principles, and maintain consistency. Like causes will always produce like effects.

Risk

In 2018, there was an article in USA Today that interviewed high net worth individuals. In this article it claimed that 61% of the people interviewed achieved their wealth by taking risks, while the other 39% claimed it was all luck. If you look at this on a deeper level, you'll see that risk was involved with the entire group because some sort of action had to be taken by the smaller percentage, and this action involved some potential risk in the hopes of a bigger payoff. Most people don't take risks because they are afraid they'll fail. The ones who are successful may have been afraid as well, but they knew that you've only truly failed if you choose not to do anything at all.

I'm not saying that you should risk everything you have on some investment with the hopes that it will work, that would be insane. What I'm saying is that if you have sufficient information on an opportunity, and the capital to support making the investment, yet you do nothing about it, then you've failed. Failed because you didn't take the necessary risk to ensure the financial success that can help you. I missed out on an opportunity some years ago because I was afraid, and mention this in *Introduction to Financial Success*.

As many of you may know, 2021 presented opportunity if you chose to seize it. The trading situation where traders were purchasing shares of AMC and GameStop presented a short-term chance to increase your capital if you got in at the right moment. I'm not saying that what those traders from the Reddit group WallStreetBets did was right, what I'm saying is that an opportunity presented itself, and some people capitalized on it. The share price on the stock market is typically a reflection of the business a company is doing. At that time, AMC and GameStop were failing due to advancements in technology, the way people were viewing movies and buying games, and because of social distancing protocols. Those companies didn't adapt quickly enough and could find themselves faltering like Blockbuster or Kodak did when Netflix, digital cameras, and cell phones with cameras came along. The select group of people who chose to trade those stocks traded on the secondary market, so the value of the shares only affect the individual trader's price, not the company's revenue as they've already received any profit from shares when it first came to the market. Eventually people realized this and the price per share fell, but those who cashed out before this happened were the real winners. In a way, I admire those traders because hedge funds have done the same thing to individual traders for years and now that the script was flipped, they're upset. Like I said, I don't condone what actually was done because it's sort of ignorance without a plan, but it's nice seeing people taking risk, even if it's more akin to gambling.

There are a myriad number of books, podcasts, and YouTube

videos that can assist you in understanding any subject more in depth related to finance. The Small Business Administration (SBA) is another useful tool. In this day and age there's no need to live a working-class life if you truly desire a better life. The day you stop learning is the day you become ignorant due to the fact that you can't learn everything about a subject. This is where you have to utilize one of your most valuable assets—time. To quote Jim Rohn, "Time is our most valuable asset, yet we tend to waste it, kill it, and spend it rather than invest it." I believe that if you invest your time wisely into learning some of the ins and outs of how to be self-made or financially successful while taking the necessary actions, then you have no choice but to reap what you sow. Simply knowing the process of getting rich or wealthy is not enough to get you there. You have to believe you can acquire self-made status, change your thoughts, develop new habits, and invest wisely in yourself.

<u>Work</u>

Most people constantly gripe about how the wealthy don't pay taxes or that they pay less tax than "ordinary" people, all the while not knowing that wealthy individuals pay roughly 70% of all taxes. The truth is that paying less taxes than you have to is legal through certain tax advantages provided by the same government that wants to raise taxes, and using the same advantages is important to becoming self-made. There are opportunities and investments galore that allow you to take advantage of tax breaks and loopholes, just like the wealthy. However, instead of making a fortune by doing some research and work, most people want to take what others have worked hard or smart for or complain about what the next person has that they don't. In today's society, people would rather sue, scam, or use others for financial gain instead of following in the footsteps of the truly successful.

It's important to note that self-made people and wealthy individuals have their money work for them and not the other way around. No one gets rich working for wages because of the vicious cycle of working to pay someone else first, mainly the government, and not paying yourself first. In essence, you're dependent on someone else providing for you instead of being your own boss. That's why you hear the axiom that it's not how much you make but how much you get to keep that will make you financially successful. Real bosses know how to make money work for them by using leverage or other people's money (OPM). They reinvest any earnings or profits they make, thus aiding the power of compounding interest.

The poor, working, and middle class all work for money on a literal and figurative level. A large majority think that money will solve all their problems, so they work harder, longer, and even take multiple jobs just to have "extra" money. Most don't realize that the more money you make as an employee, the more Uncle Sam will take, and this could put you in a higher tax bracket. I learned in the military that the government will give you $100 and take back $99, which is true on a certain level. It took some adversity for me to learn why investing in an education, especially a financial one, is important.

Certain economic classes are also the ones buying things with no real value just to keep up with the Kardashians or to look the part of having money. I know because I was one of those people, "flexing for the Gram." This I-have-to-look-rich mentality affects many of us who grew up not knowing the power of money and finance, which keeps the majority of us in the same place our parents and possibly grandparents were in for generations. Money is their master because it tells them when to get up and go to work, and it keeps them in the rat race where they never learn to take calculated risks and forever remaining an employee.

If you want to change your outlook and become a self-made boss, then you're in the right place. I, too, have been in the rat race and got tired of that shit. It took me hitting rock bottom, reevaluating my life, and investing in myself before I learned how to boss up. This is how *Self-Made* and *The Money Master Series* were born. This book will introduce you to some of the investments that you can use in a self-directed IRA (SDIRA) that aren't allowed through traditional IRAs or employer sponsored retirement plans. There are many ways to become self-made and I'm only showing you one. By no means does my knowledge base encompass the subject within as a whole, and I am not a financial expert, however, the information I'll provide is in as simple a format as I comprehend so that you can go out and try your hand at becoming self-made. If you're tired of waiting on someone to give you a paycheck or seeing your retirement accounts grow slowly while paying high fees, and you're ready to get in your bag, then turn the page and start your own self-made journey.

CONTENTS

CHAPTER ONE:
UNDERSTANDING THE PRINCIPLES OF FINANCE

———————— ⊸∘〰〰∘⊶ ————————

"I don't get mad. I just get money" – Young Jeezy, *Bottom of the Map*

If I told you that I was giving you $1,000,000, what would you do with it? Like most people, your initial reaction might be to spend it. Now, what if I changed the terms and said, "I'm giving you $1,000,000, but in order to keep it, you have to turn it into $2,000,000 within 90 days or I'll take the $1,000,000." What would you do then? I ask this because the first situation causes your mind to think from a consumer perspective while the second should cause you to think from an investor or business perspective. As for the first question, a few years ago I would have thought of purchasing a McLaren

570GT Coupe and updating my wardrobe, but that was before I learned about finance and how to think like an investor or producer. The simple answer to the second question is to deposit it into a bank and ask for a $1,000,000 loan and if you're smart, you would repeat this step with another bank. All I ask is that you don't repeat this with other banks just to blow the funds on consumer products like a "Lambo" or a big house just to impress your friends. You should look to invest it in purchasing assets that appreciate and provide cash flow, which is part of the reason for this publication. I want to get you into a mindset of thinking, "how can I afford that," instead of purchasing it outright with no way to offset cost.

My journey into the world of finance began close to a decade ago. I had over $60,000 in consumer debt (bad debt), little to no savings, and a small retirement account with less than $2,500 after seven years of military service. To top it off, I was married and supporting six children. My original goal was to make a career of the Army and "retire at the age of forty with twenty-two years of service, but some bad choices in life altered that course. This turned out to be a blessing in disguise though because I ended up on the path of becoming my own boss (selfmade, baby!) and took charge of my own retirement. By understanding and applying the knowledge in this book, you too will be able to become your own boss one day. Now let's get into the first part of this book.

There are experts and gurus who teach or explain that we should invest, whether that is in a 401(k), Individual Retirement Account (IRA), or some other form of a defined contribution plan, such as a 403 (b) where we are put in charge of our own financial destiny and in a way forced to navigate the complicated world of finance and capital markets. In my studies I have rarely seen those same people discuss the 'why' and explain the principles that guide finance so that almost anyone can grasp the concepts of their money. In this chapter I will do just that—explain the five principles of finance. By learning and applying these principles to your investment strategies, you should be better able to bridge the wealth gap, or at least secure a more financially stable future for yourself and your family, if you so choose.

The first principle of finance that you need to grasp is that *money has time value*. What this means is that a dollar today is worth more than one received tomorrow. This principle works conversely in that a dollar received tomorrow is worth less than one received today. This is due to the ability of money received today being able to earn interest, which makes money today more valuable. For instance, imagine that you did not need money and had a choice of receiving $5,000 today or waiting five years to receive $6,500. By not necessarily needing the money today, some people would opt to receive the higher amount at a later date. That is fine and dandy, however, it would ignore the principle being discussed. Why? Because you are able to utilize the funds today and invest it to earn interest. Let's say that you take the $5,000 and invest it in an index fund that returns annualized 7 percent. By holding this investment for five years, the same as you would have to wait to receive the $6,500, you allow your value to grow to over $7,000 because your original $5,000 earned interest, and that interest earned interest—the power of compounding. However, if you waited five years to receive the $6,500, you missed out on that opportunity to earn interest and you lose buying power because of inflation or the rise in the price of goods. That means that instead of having the buying power of $6,500 your buying power is close to $5,600 five years ago, accounting for inflation at 3 percent.

When we first start working, we believe that we have nothing but time on our hands or that we can invest later when we earn more. By doing this we suffer from what is called *opportunity loss* or *opportunity cost*. The cycle of working, paying taxes, spending, and repeat is how the majority live their lives for a few decades of fun and labor instead of paying themselves first and when it comes close to retirement time they try to play catch up (insanity anyone?). By understanding the principles outlined in this chapter, we are able to put aside a set amount to ensure that we will be able to enjoy life later on because we will produce cash flow. In order to do this though we must first practice self-control and avoid consumption (save). Milton Friedman stated it best in his book *Money Mischief* where he says, "Accumulating an asset requires saving, that is avoiding consumption. Once the asset is accumulated, it may cost something to maintain, as with physical inventories, or it may yield a return in the form of a flow of income, such as interest on a mortgage or bond or dividends on stocks" (p.25). Basically, we should look to be producers of cash flow instead of just consumers of goods, thus allowing us to both spend and earn to help offset the cost of each. Now back to this thing of opportunity cost.

Recall that the first principle of finance it that money has time value. Money represents value but has no value itself. What I mean is that money is only a representative of the value for other things we can get with it. It makes it easy to value goods and services so that we don't have to spend time bartering for basic necessities like in the olden days. With the previous example of receiving $5,000 today or $6,500 in five years I stated that you would suffer from opportunity cost or what some call opportunity loss. This means that we forego an alternative by choosing or making a decision to purchase one thing over another. To break this down further, what this can also mean is that just because we can do almost anything with money doesn't mean that we can do everything.

Opportunity cost, or loss, means that we must make choices, sacrifices, and we have to decide which things we will or won't do. An example of this was being given an allowance as a child. My mother used to give us an allowance of $5 back in the day when that was a decent amount of money. During the school year there was a snack bar where we could purchase items while on break. It was hard for a kid not to buy something when your friends and other kids were eating their candy and drinking sodas, so I spent my allowance on snacks as well. I did this for quite some time until I realized just how much we loved our snacks, so I came up with the idea to sell my own snacks. Whenever we would take our weekly trip to Wal-Mart, I would purchase a few bags of Kiddie Mix assorted candies that included Tootsie Rolls, Sweetarts, and other candies for around $5. I also purchased Zip-lock bags, which caused me to borrow from my parents. I bagged up the candies into $0.50 and $1 baggies and sold them at school; I even employed my younger sisters to help me move my product and paid them. I was making about $20 off one bag of Kiddie Mix. This is a classic example of opportunity cost by foregoing consumption of school snacks and instead choosing to become a supplier of goods that returned dividends. Opportunity cost can be seen throughout this story if you look at it and is the basis for principle one.

Before we move on to principle two, I would like to give you a different example of money having time value in another sense just in case you are still lost. I recall one time as a youth when we assumed my mother had lost the car keys while we were shopping at good old Wally World. My sisters and I, along with our parents, walked every aisle looking for those keys. We had no such luck, so they paid for the groceries and we walked to the car. Our stepfather was upset, and it was funny; he was known for saying something outrageous. To add to the situation, when we got to the car, he saw the keys in the ignition, but the doors were locked. We tried for a while to break-in, but nothing worked. We tried jury rigging stuff, using our small hands, and just about anything our country father could think of. Eventually we had to call a locksmith who charged $75 to get into the car and it only took him 2-3 minutes to complete the job. What I am saying in this example is that this man's time was valued at $75, whether the job was for those 2- 3 minutes or for an hour. Some people may feel that is steep, but if he took the whole hour to complete the job would that make the value of our time, yours, or his seem reasonable? This question brings us to our second principle of finance.

Principle two of finance is *there is a risk-reward tradeoff.* This means that we will not take any additional risk unless we expect to be compensated a higher return for doing so. In my previous example involving the locksmith, my parents risked losing several things such as time, sleep, and travel time home by trying to get into the car on their own. Instead they gave up funds in order to be rewarded their time back. I discuss different investments that have risk-reward tradeoff in my book *Introduction to Financial Success,* and I will get into some of the same investments in chapter two. As far as risk-reward is concerned, it is easier if you think in terms of pros (reward) and cons (risk). For the record, please don't mistake risk for gambling. The major difference between the two is knowing when to cut your losses. My old man used to tell me that a short-term defeat is better than a long-term disaster. When dealing with risk, if you lose you are able to recover and possibly return to your original position with acceptable losses. On the other hand, with a gamble a defeat can lead to mounting problems that are likely to spiral out of control, much similar to an addiction.

Growing up in certain economic classes, one is likely to see others of the same class engage in certain games of chance in hopes of winning some prize, mainly money. These certain people are lured by the chance of easy money and are further drawn in by their emotions. These games can include your state lottery program, scratch-offs, raffle games, slot machines, or anything where people can wager money in hopes of winning a larger pot such as card games (Tunk or Spades), dominoes, dice, and let's not forget good ole BINGO! I had a female friend who gambled with her family by playing cards every first of the month like clockwork. Last time I checked, this is still going on and I've known her for over 15 years. The pot for playing is by no means small. It can get up to $50 a hand if you're betting on everything, i.e. low spade, lowest hand, or whatever you fancy. To top it off, if a person "tunks," you're out $20 for that pot instead of the original $10 plus anything you lost on side bets. My lady friend also had a thing for the slot machine as well. I am not without fault and I won't just talk about others because I've gambled once or twice in my life.

I was a young twenty-year-old who was visiting home from my duty station in Alaska with my wife and kids. There was some sort of carnival going on at one of the local shopping plazas and it had games and rides. There was a game of chance with ring toss that I was lured into. I got caught up in the thought of winning more money and didn't consider the money I could, and eventually would, lose. The prize eventually rose to $1,000 and I could've won if I placed one more ring in the center. I kept getting close, which caused me to keep spending. I eventually lost $200 chasing that prize. Looking back, I see different ways I could've came out on top or broke even. (Hint: negotiation skills are a must in life). Through this I learned that gambling can put you in a position where you try harder to rescue the situation, i.e. spending more money to break even or playing catchup, and you often end up making the situation worse or sinking deeper into a hole. A gamble just has too many variables that can complicate things down the road, unlike a risk which has variables you can control.

When I was learning about how insurance worked, I learned ways to control risk. These big businesses used a technique called ARRT or avoid, reduce, retain, or transfer. These are simple techniques and can be done by mostly anyone. Avoiding risk simply means not taking the risk when the rewards don't justify doing so. You reduce your risk by lowering the loss from happening, which gives you the most personal control. Retaining risk means you pay any losses out of pocket, i.e., deductibles, and you transfer the risk by shifting it to someone else or splitting it amongst yourself and other parties. By utilizing these concepts, you can create what is known as asymmetrical risk/reward. This can be instrumental in becoming your own boss. There are products and opportunities that are out there for the ultra-wealthy that have limited risk exposure with big rewards because of these same principles. I will get into some of the asymmetrical risk/reward products that can be used by those not ultra-wealthy in chapter two.

There are many businessmen, women, and investors that I admire. Their bodies of work speak volumes and many of them have changed the game in their lane. A few of my favorite people include Tyler Perry, Oprah Winfrey, Sir Richard Branson, Anthony "Tony" Robbins, Robert Kiyosaki, and recently, Deborah Razo. I admire these individuals because they understand the concept of risk/reward and the power of investing in yourself. One of Sir Branson's important phrases in life is, "protect the downside." If you don't know, Sir Richard Branson is the owner of Virgin Brands. He is the consummate example of how creating asymmetrical risk/reward can be a wealth maker. His story began back in the 1980s with his launch of Virgin Airways. Somehow, he managed to purchase his first five aircrafts with the option to return them if things didn't work out, unheard of at the time. Through this deal it meant that if he failed, he would not lose, however if he won then he won big. We all know how that turned out as he has built a billion-dollar empire. Sir Richard Branson 's story portrays one of risking a little to win to make a lot. If you truly want to take risk/reward to heart, then you should strive to live by Warren Buffet's mantra for investing, "Rule 1: Don't lose money and Rule 2: See rule 1."

Sir Francis Bacon told us that money makes a good servant but a bad master. Many people don't realize that money is a tool or means to an end, not an end in itself. Money is vital, but not paramount for everything in life, yet people will lie for it, steal it, and even kill for it. For some people it's a taboo subject, much like politics or religion. It's one of those things you don't talk about with family, friends, or strangers. This seems crazy considering that some people give their health, time, and even family for this thing called money all because its valued more highly than the things given up. This brings me to the third principle of finance: *cash flows are the source of value.*

Cash flows are the source of value because they represent money that can be spent, and it's what determines an investments value, such as in real estate or the valuation of a business for sale. It's important not to confuse cash flow with profits because they are completely different. Profit measures performance over an interval of time and is how accountants make judgments of a business' costs and revenues. It's possible for a business to show a profit on paper but generate no cash flow. Maybe you've heard of such companies as many new upstarts stay in this stage for years before showing positive cash flow. Negative cash flow occurs when expenses exceed your profits and causes a business to operate in the red, or at a loss. A profit is based on revenues or how the company earned its income through incurred expenses, it's money taken into account before any interest and taxes are paid. Cash flows, on the other hand, is what's left and can be spent. If that is confusing, I'll provide you examples here shortly.

There are four types of financial statements: income statement, balance sheet, statement of cash flows, and statement of shareholder's equity. I will go over the first two types for the purpose of this book and the following examples. An income statement, for accounting purposes, deals with revenues earned over a specific period of time, the expenses incurred to earn the revenues, and profit earned. It helps to think of this as either your pay stub or end of the year tax statement. A balance sheet gives you information, as of the date prepared, about any assets, liabilities, and equity. If you've ever balanced a checkbook, then this is similar with the exception of assets, liabilities, and equity.

Imagine that you own a convenience store and it's the end of the year. You've been keeping your own books and it's time to prepare an income statement to see how well you've done for the year ending 2020. You look at all business for the year and see that you had revenues that totaled $2,700,000 for the whole year or twelve-month period ending December 31, 2020. This is going well, so you continue with creating your income statement. Next you see that your store incurred various expenses to produce this revenue. For one, you see that you spent $2,125,000 to acquire goods that were sold. Also, during the year, you had operating expenses, like electric bills, salaries, administrative costs, etc., that totaled $364,075. You couldn't finance these costs alone, so you borrowed funds from your local bank and paid out interest fees that totaled $67,500. Don't forget that you owe taxes on this revenue and your rate is 34 percent. Considering all the information contained here, your income statement would look as such:

Income Statement for year ending December 31, 2020	
Revenues (sales)	$2,700,000
Cost of Goods	($2,125,000)
Gross Profit	$575,000
Operating Expense	($364,075)
Net Operating Income	$210,925
Interest Expense	($67,500)
Income Tax @ 34%	($48,764.50)
Net Income	$94,660.50

I'm going to explain what all this means, but it all boils

down to the difference between profits and cash flow which I mentioned in the beginning of principle three. It was probably easier to state that revenues, or sales, minus expenses equal profit, but then you may not have seen the bigger picture that I wanted you to see.

Revenues or sales for the year totaled $2.7 million and it's the cumulative dollar amount of goods sold to your customers for that period. In order to produce the income, you needed goods to sell, which costs money. The total amount that you spent to acquire those goods came to $2.125 million. By subtracting your cost of goods from your sales you are left with your profit; this is how your business produces its cash flow and represents money that can't be freely spent. As you can see from the income statement, you still need to account for other operating costs, interest owed, and your tax obligations before you get to the bottom line or cash flow. So, for the year ending December 31, 2020 you had a yearly net income of $94,660.50 or $7,888.38 in cash flow on a monthly basis. Once again, cash flows are the source of value. This is extremely important because later on I will discuss real estate as a way to become self-made and the cash flow from your properties will be a defining factor.

If you think about it an income statement and balance sheet go hand-in-hand. An income statement deals with revenues (sales) and expenses, while a balance sheet deals with assets, liabilities, and equity. An asset produces revenues or income that has expense or liabilities. Your equity is the income left after all expenses have been paid or money already invested if you used debt and equity. Real estate is a great example of what I mean by this, and is one of the keys that will make you self-made. I'll provide you with a few examples of how the income statement and balance sheet work in unison.

Let's say that you own a duplex (asset) and you used a loan from the bank to finance 80 percent of the cost. You put up $37,500 in equity in order to get this asset that's valued at $187,500; this makes your loan $150,000. The monthly payments for this loan in $800 and is spread out over 30 years, and you rent both units for $650 a month. Based on this alone your profit is $500. The only other expenses you have are insurance and taxes which total $450. After all this is said and done, you are left with $50 as your cash flow at the end of the month. What you end up with is a loan for $150,000 (a liability that shows up on your balance sheet) that helped purchase a duplex (an asset on your balance sheet) that produces $50 (income on your income statement) after paying $450 (expenses on your income statement) in expenses.

A simple representation would be as such:
Income Statement

Income $50
Expenses $450

Balance Sheet

Asset Duplex (value $187,500)
Liability $150,000 loan
Equity $37,500

This next example is one that involves me. Thus far this is

my second book, and it costs money to have this thing edited, printed, and published. After all of this is done, I still need to make sales. Let's say that my publishing company receives offers to sell my works overseas in 15 countries and receives $3,000 per license. My cost to get this to market ran $5,000 before I get to collect. With the licenses I get $45,000 from international sales, less the $5,000 in expenses, for a total of $40,000 in net income plus royalties from all the books sold around the world. Not a bad payday, right? My income statement would include $40,000 from licensing plus royalties with expenses totaling $5,000 initially. My balance sheet would include this book as an asset with no liabilities. The two financial statements work in unison and they give you a picture of yourself or your business.

Income Statement

| Income $40,000 plus Royalties @xx% |
| Expenses $5,000 |

Balance Sheet

| Asset *Self-Made: How to Invest in Yourself* (Book) |
| Liabilities |

This is what both of my financial statements would look like in simple terms. By now you should have a decent grasp on how and why cash flows are the source of value. If not, then I suggest you reread this section as many times as necessary. Remember, cash flows are the source of value, income statements deal with income and expenses, and balance sheets deal with assets and liabilities. Also, profits are good but represent how expenses and revenues (sales) are allocated while cash flow is money that can actually be spent.

If money wasn't a factor and you had a choice between paying $50 for a pair of nondescript jeans and paying $150 for designer jeans, which would you choose? The majority would probably choose the designer jeans because we tend to think that price represents value. Add to this advertising about high fashion and we begin to value the designer jeans more highly because a popular artist is wearing or talking about it. Economists tend to avoid this sort of judgment through what is known as the diamond water paradox. It is said that this paradox extends back to Adam Smith and his famous work *The Wealth of Nations* where he distinguishes between what's called *value in use* and *value in exchange.*

Value in exchange and value in use don't always line up. For example, a diamond has great value in exchange because you can get a lot for it if you were to trade it. However, it doesn't have much value in use like water does. What I mean by this is that we don't go around eating or drinking diamonds like we do water in its various forms. Basically, diamonds are a luxury item and are seen as frivolous. Water is a basic necessity of life and has much use like transportation, cooking, or hydroelectricity. Water has a high value in use but a low value in exchange considering how inexpensive it is, and the fact that you can get it for free through rain. Overall, diamonds have a high price because they are scarce, people want them, and are willing to pay a high price for them. This brings us to the fourth principle of finance: *market price reflects information.*

This principle is based on how investors respond to new

information when buying and selling their investments. In essence these investments are marked-to-market meaning that in efficient markets, such as the United States and other developed countries, price increases have already been taken into consideration by the markets because investors have already anticipated any new information released. It is safe to say that the market determines prices, not any producer of goods or services. Consider the price of gasoline for example. If people are driving, buying expensive SUVs, and traveling around the world in large droves, then the big oil companies can afford to raise prices to cover costs, such as drilling for new sites. This is due to the market giving information such as '5 million people are expected to hit the road during the first week of summer with numbers increasing dramatically,' or reports that there's been a large uptick in the purchase of SUVs (gas guzzlers). On the flip side, if the same oil companies tried to raise prices when travel was down or information surfaced that more people are purchasing fuel efficient vehicles, then the high fuel prices wouldn't suffice, and prices would have to drop. Yes, the oil companies want to make the most money, but supply and demand will determine price.

The fifth and final principle of finance is that *individuals respond to incentives*. We all like to be rewarded for doing a good job, achieving a goal, or given recognition. Even animals respond well to incentives, i.e. belly rubs or treats. Corporations and governments know and use this principle well. Do you travel a lot? How about air miles or lounge privileges as an incentive to use certain credit cards or to encourage you to continue traveling? Cash back is another incentive employed by businesses. There are businesses that incentivize employees for meeting goals, which can be both good and bad, especially if those incentives don't align with shareholder value. If those incentives don't match said shareholder values, then managers and employees may make decisions that are not increasing value. Take Wells Fargo and how, a few years ago, several accounts were created in customers name just so sales goals could be met and incentives earned; or how in the early 2000s, lenders gave out NINJA (no income, no job) loans for homes without properly screening the applicants and then sold those loans as MBSs (Mortgage-Backed Securities). The latter incident led to the Great Recession of 2008 and as for the Wells Fargo situation, employees only did what was ordered by upper management, yet the employees were the ones who suffered most. This is a form of agency problem where management goals are not aligned with creating shareholder value or keeping to the company vision. The bank ended up being fined a few hundred million dollars while making billions in a single quarter. This was a slap on the wrist and not an admission of guilt.

Governments employ incentives as well in order to get people to do its bidding. They incentivize programs they want to encourage and tax those they want to discourage. Solar energy, affordable housing, and investment in opportunity zones all carry some sort of incentive from the government because they are all great for society and keeps governments from having to invest fully in the program by itself. On the flip side, most governments have a mindset of "give them fish" rather than "teach them to fish" when it comes to assisting people. Programs such as Temporary Assistance for Needy Families (TANF) and the Earned Income Credit (EIC) were created to help low-income families *temporarily*, but it has given people a cop out. There are those who exploit these programs because of the "free money." Programs like food stamps, welfare, and Medicare have become staples of low-income families and many people consciously choose to stay in that comfortable buffer and collect those government benefits. I'm sure many of you either know someone like this or at least have heard of someone. This is allowed to continue because people in politics think that no one willingly abuses or exploits the system. I'm not saying everyone does this. Hell, my family was once on government assistance, but my mother worked her ass off and we no longer needed those programs. She probably could have exploited the system as a working woman with four children and hardly any other assistance, but she wanted better for herself and her kids.

Incentives are not all bad or all good; there's always a trade-off. If you look at the five principles, you may notice that principle two and five are closely related. In principle two I talk about people not taking on additional risk unless they expect to be compensated. Incentives are a form of compensation in order to take that risk. Offering a higher rate of interest on a junk bond is an incentive for people to invest. Imagine that you have $1,000 and you had a choice between saving it at your local bank and earning 0.005 percent a year or investing that same $1,000 in a company that needed financing and offered a corporate bond that gives a rate of 15 percent for five years, what will you choose? The savings account is the safe bet because it's backed by the Federal Depository Insurance Company (FDIC), but the bond is extremely risky and backed by a desperate company that could give you a great return or you could lose your principle. For some people the choice is easy, while others may find it tough. It all depends on your tolerance for risk and your understanding of the markets, which is the subject of the next chapter.

In conclusion, there are five basic principles of finance that you need to be familiar with in order to gain financial literacy and be on your way to self-made status. The first principle is that *money has time value*. This means that money today is worth more than money received tomorrow because of its ability to be invested and earn interest. The second principle is that *there's a risk/reward tradeoff*. People won't take additional risk unless they expect to be compensated for doing so, unless you're some sort of adrenaline junkie and enjoy taking risk just because. *Cash flow as the source of value* is our third principle. Cash flows represent money that can be freely spent and is free from any liabilities such as taxes or interest, unlike profits. Any time you see the price of a security, such as stocks, the market has priced in all information because people have already anticipated any new information that's been put out, this is the basis of principle four. This is important information if you want to invest or trade the markets. Finally, *people respond to incentives* is fifth principle and means that we enjoy being compensated or acknowledged for taking risk. Keep these principles in mind because they will continue to guide you throughout this book as they will allow you to see how certain securities respond to each principle or multiple principles. Now, let's learn about the financial marketplace and markets.

CHAPTER TWO:
FINANCIAL MARKETS AND
MARKETPLACES

—————◄◦⌒⌒◦►—————

"Financial freedom my only hope…Fuck livin' rich and dyin'
broke." – Jay-Z, *The Story of OJ, 4:44 Album*

Y ou may be someone living paycheck to paycheck or
know someone in that situation, and the last few
economic hiccups haven't helped your situation—
recession of 2008 or the Covid-19 pandemic. Those who
saved have most likely drawn from that savings and maybe
even taken from a retirement account. Others may have had to
depend on economic stimulus from the government or been
"fortunate" enough to have an essential job that provided
continued financial support. Whatever's the case, now is the
time to start preparing yourself financially to withstand another

economic downturn if, and when, it comes. This begins with getting literate on finance and learning how to play the game like millions before you. This chapter will introduce you to financial markets and marketplaces as well as some of the securities that can be used to pursue and maintain your path to financial freedom and boss status.

A financial market is any place where money and credit are exchanged. Within these markets there are three principal sets of players: **savers, borrowers, and financial institutions**. Business courses teach that savers are people who have money to invest and can be saving money for a number of reasons. A business can also save excess cash in reserves for later purchase of equipment or for acquisitions. According to my business courses, the savers are considered investors, however, I believe in the Rich Dad school of thought where savers aren't investors. If all a person does is save for, let's say a down payment for a home or car, then that person is not truly an investor. Like Robert Kiyosaki, I believe savers to be losers because the borrowers, at least the ones who invest in assets, and the financial institutions will make more off of the funds being saved than the saver. I will explain this in greater detail later on, so for now I will continue to focus on the principal players in the markets. Borrowers are those who need money to finance their purchases. These individuals may need money to finance investments or purchase new inventory. Borrowers may also need funds to purchase consumer debt such as a car, furniture, or to pay down credit card debt. Those who use it for the aforementioned (investments or new inventory) are the true investors. Financial institutions, or intermediaries, help bring borrowers and savers together. These institutions include commercial banks, insurance companies, investment companies, finance companies, and investment banks.

Commercial banks are something we're all familiar with as they are the ones that accept our loans and deposits and allow us use of those funds via a checking account. Businesses tend to hit up these types of financial institutions first before considering other intermediaries. One-way commercial banks make money is by lending to borrowers at an interest rate that far exceeds the rate they pay savers. These banks tend to be ranked by the total dollar value of their deposits and most of these large banks are owned by holding companies that also hold other types of businesses. The Big Four in the United States, at last check, are the Bank of America Corporation, JPMorgan Chase and Company, Wells Fargo Bank, and Citigroup Inc.

Insurance companies, by definition, are in the business of selling insurance to individuals and businesses to protect their investments. These companies collect premiums and hold them in reserve accounts until there's an insured loss and they will play an important part in some securities that will be discussed later. Once a loss happens, the company pays out claims to the holder(s) of the insurance contract. You have companies such as American International Group (AIG) or Prudential that build up huge pools of reserves, like a mutual fund, and those reserves are used to make various types of investments (loans) and pay claims. Some of these companies engage in services such as consumer finance, aircraft and equipment leasing, and debt and loan insurance. You may recognize the latter service by another name as it was part of the reason for the economic recession in 2008. This particular transaction is known as a credit default swap and they act like an insurance policy in that they pay out if a particular bond or security defaults.

Investment companies include mutual funds, hedge funds, and private equity firms. These are all institutions that pool the savings of individuals and invest the money in securities issued by other companies. A mutual fund can invest in virtually all the securities offered in the financial markets. Each fund is a standalone company that contracts with an investment manager who takes the funds and buys securities on the behalf of investors. Mutual funds will be discussed in more detail later on along with other types of investments. Hedge funds are similar to a mutual fund but have less regulation and more risk. In order to invest in one, you have to be an accredited investor which means that you have a net worth in excess of $1,000,000 or make $200,000 ($300,000, if married) per year. This can include individuals, corporations, and retirement plans.

Private equity firms are another type of investment company and they invest in equities that aren't traded on the public markets. There are two types of firms that dominate this group and you may have heard of one or both—venture capital firms (VC) and leveraged buyout firms (LBO). Venture capitalists are those who raise money from investors, either wealthy people or financial institutions, and use the funds for financing private start-up companies by first round financing. Think *Shark Tank* and what those wealthy individuals do for companies. These firms get in on the action before the public even knows about it, hence the "private" of private equity. LBOs acquire established firms that haven't been performing well. These firms do this with the goal of making the businesses profitable once more and selling them later. There are movies that have been made about such companies and, if you're curious, I suggest watching *Barbarians at the Gate* or *Other People's Money* as a starting point. Overall, private equity funding plays

CARLING D. COLBERT, SR.

a major part in financing new businesses and underwriting the renovation of old and faltering ones. The next section will discuss the financial marketplace and securities that you can use to help create cash flow and build long term wealth aka, boss status.

The Financial Marketplace

When engaged in the financial marketplace, you tend to deal with what is known as 'securities.' A security is simply some negotiable instrument that represents a financial claim. This can mean stocks or some other debt agreement such as a T-bill (Treasury bill). Securities markets are usually discussed in terms of primary and secondary markets, while the types of securities fall into two basic categories: **debt and equity**. A primary market is one where new securities are bought and sold for the first time. This type of market allows firms to issue securities to raise money that can be used to finance their businesses. The firms actually receive the money raised from primary markets, unlike funds in the secondary market. In the secondary market, securities are transferred from one investor to another investor, and doesn't allow the issuing firm to receive any new financing from the transaction. The secondary market allows us liquidity or the ability to convert a security to cash quickly if we decide we no longer wanted to hold shares of some company, such as Blockbuster or Game Stop.

If you're like me, or most people for that matter, you know a thing or two about debt. Usually you borrow funds from a person or an institution, such as a bank, to make a purchase and the funds must be repaid along with interest. It's no different for businesses that want to borrow money. Businesses that want to borrow money do so by selling debt securities in the debt market. This can be in the money markets or capital markets. Money markets are known as short-term debt and must be repaid in less than one year while capital markets refer to long-term financial instruments such as bonds. Debt is cheaper to finance than equity because debt can be sold or refinanced, but for some firms issuing equity securities may be the only way. Two types of equity securities are common stock and preferred stock. I will discuss each type momentarily, but before I get into that I'd like to identify the different type of financial securities that you may come in contact with in the markets.

The majority of the securities that will be identified will not get you to boss status alone, most are just a starting point or a way to diversify you holdings, so don't go out and start purchasing them and expect to immediately get rich. First, I will begin with identifying money market debt and some of the instruments that make up this market. Afterwards, I will give you a few long-term debt and fixed income securities to round out the markets. Finally, to cap this chapter off, I will give you some information on other instruments you can participate in that aren't listed in a typical financial course and can help you as well.

In the money markets, as an investor, you typically get low returns that tend to be close to the rate of inflation, you get safety (low risk/low reward), and you get high liquidity. Earlier it was mentioned that in debt markets the money that is borrowed must be repaid within one year or less and the instruments that will be listed here mature within that timeframe. You can purchase Treasury bills (T-bills), negotiable certificates of deposits, money market mutual funds, or consumer credit in this market, just to name a few. Most of them require you to be an accredited investor and are simply listed because if you follow the information in later chapters, you will eventually get there, as well as following information in *Introduction to Financial Success*, which gives you a variety of ways to get in your bag.

For instance, U.S. Treasury bills are instruments you can invest in without being an accredited investor, while consumer credit, in particular credit card debt, requires you to be. T-bills are government debt obligations issued by the U.S. Treasury that can come due or mature between four weeks to one year. They are the basis for most short-term bond index funds and money market funds. Technically speaking, T-bills, notes, and bonds are all considered bonds and are backed by the full faith and credit of the U.S. Government, which is why they are so safe and have such a low rate of return. The only major difference between the three is the wait time for collecting your principal. T-bills are usually sold at a discount and allow you to get full value at maturity. The minimum investment for all three is $1,000 and, on the off chance you get a T-bill at a discounted price of 96 or $960 you will collect $1,000 when it mature which ends up being a return of four percent.

Credit card debt is fairly new to me and is beyond the scope of this book. I stumbled across this market after reviewing old credit reports and browsing my old textbooks. I will attempt to give you a glimpse of this market based on what I know, however, you should conduct your own due diligence on this subject.

Buying credit card debt is a market that requires you to be an accredited investor. Entering this field may be a long-term goal and can be a way to diversify your holdings. I believe this is a well-kept secret because I wasn't aware that this was a thing until I looked over old credit reports and saw that an old credit

card account had been purchased by a debt buyer some
years ago. This caused me to want to know more on the
subject and how I too could profit from it in the future.
Through my short research I learned this debt is unsecured,
meaning that there's no collateral or assets to help secure
payment. This makes it difficult for you to collect or enforce
the debt. However, in some states this debt can be converted
to a secured debt under certain circumstances: 1) the debtor
owns real estate; 2) a collection lawsuit results in a judgment;
or 3) the judgment gets documented as a lien. The credit card
companies that usually sell the debt do so in multimillion
dollar pools. The debt is sold at a discount (between 5-20%)
but it doesn't hurt them because they still receive their high
interest rates from all accounts that are in good standing, which
account for roughly 90 percent of credit cards not sold off.
Anyhow, if the debt is converted into secured debt under the
listed circumstances, you increase the chances of getting paid.
Your lien may still be a low priority, but your chances are still
higher than purchasing the debt unsecured. You get variable
risk, maturity, and rates of return in this market.

When the time comes and you meet the requirement to
enter this market, you should contact a reseller to apply as an
approved buyer. This is similar to applying for a job or benefits,
you're simply filling out the application of the seller so that
they can identify you throughout certain processes. Last time
I checked it said that The Debt Buyers Association was the
leader in the field of resellers. By looking online there should
be local buyers and sellers in your region that you can contact.
After you've registered it's time to review the portfolios. During
this time, you should request this from your reseller because
there's not set format that all use. You will typically get a format

that include information such as the name of the credit card company, the account number, applicable interest rate, and the county or municipality of where the person owing the debt lives. This is not an exhaustive list, just a reference of what you can expect to find when conducting your review. The only thing I don't like about this is that you get peoples' full name, address, and social once you make a purchase agreement on the size and price. I personally don't want to be responsible for any leaks or hacks from my business computer. Besides that, this field can provide you with a high return, you can manage risk through presale due diligence, and if you can get settlements with the debtors, you'll generate a nice cash flow. I'm not advocating that you enter this particular market, however, it is something to consider helping spread your risk in the long run. I'm by far no expert, so if you want to know more on this subject then I suggest starting with *The Investor's Guide to Buying Debt* by Richard L. Shell and John P. Pratt.

Both T-bills and consumer credit fall into the debt/money market and are short-term instruments. Now it's time to learn about a few long-term debt securities. This market can help generate a dependable income and usually, but not always, produce higher returns than short term debt. For some investors' long-term debt and fixed income securities allow them to lock in an interest rate so they know their future returns, assuming that there's no default on the issuing entity's behalf. Instruments in this field include federal agency debt, U.S. Treasury notes and bonds, and corporate bonds.

U.S. Treasury notes and bonds are issued by the U.S. Government to mutual funds, businesses, and others. Notes tend to have a maturity from two to ten years while bonds are longer termed securities that mature at ten years or more.

Unlike their cousin, T-bills, these investments are sold at face value and have a fixed rate that gives you interest payments every six months. Investments issued by the U.S. Government are known as investment grade bonds because they have very little risk of defaulting unlike high-yield or "junk" bonds, which carry a relatively high risk of defaulting. Federal agency bonds tend to be investment grade as well due to them being government sponsored enterprises (GSE). This means that these corporations were created by Congress to work for the common good but do things their own way. The Federal Home Loan Mortgage Corporation, Federal National Mortgage Association, and Government National Mortgage all fall into this category. You may know these agencies by their street name of Freddie Mac, Fannie Mae, and Ginnie Mae, respectively. These bonds are also known as mortgage-backed securities (MBS) or asset-backed securities (ABS). An ABS is a bond that is secured by an asset, i.e. mortgage, in essence making a MBS a type of ABS.

The Federal Home Loan Mortgage Corporation (Freddie Mac) was formed in 1970 and is similar to the Federal National Mortgage Association (Fannie Mae). Like most of the big banks that were bailed out during the recession of 2008, this corporation is considered amongst the "too big to fail" businesses. Freddie Mac bonds are issued in increments of $1,000 like most bonds, and can be a traditional bond or a MBS. This agency finances roughly one in six homes when it buys a residential mortgage and if you'd like more information on this agency check out www.freddiemac.com

Fannie Mae began circa 1968 and raises money by selling bonds that it then releases to banks, the money that is. The banks then use the money to make loans to homebuyers.

These bonds are generally issued in $1,000 increments and are mainly purchased by other national central banks, insurance companies, and sometimes university endowment funds. You can find out more at www.fanniemae.com.

Ginnie Mae is guaranteed by the federal government and has no risk of default. This agency helps ensure that mortgage loans are readily available throughout the country. Unlike Fannie Mae and Freddie Mac, these bonds tend to be sold in $25,000 increments. Don't worry though because these bonds can be purchased for less on the secondary market as they get closer to the maturity date or as they are paid down. If that doesn't work for you, then you can get a Ginnie Mae mutual fund or exchange traded fund (ETF), however, these are significantly different than an individual bond. To purchase any of these agency bonds all you need to do is contact a broker or financial advisor. If you'd like to get a more general knowledge of these securities check out, *Mortgage-Backed Securities* by Justin Adams. I will also be putting out more information on investing in part II of my *Money Master* series to be titled *Introduction to Financial Success on Investing.*

A third major issuer of bonds are corporations. Corporate bonds are issued by corporations to individuals and institutional investors. These bonds tend to be riskier than government and agency bonds, so investors are compensated by being given a higher rate of interest. These corporations issue bonds when they want to raise money to expand, pay dividends, or a host of other reasons. Generally corporate bonds pay one percentage point higher than U.S. Treasuries. The risk involved with some corporate bonds depends on the financial strength of the issuer. Bonds will not get you to boss status alone, however, they do help add diversity and stability while traveling the boss path. The quality of any bond is based on its ratings, whether that's AAA or D grade by raters such as Moody's or Standard & Poor's (S&P). This helps you weigh the risk/reward of the bond and is what good investing is about.

Thus far I've discussed debt securities and some of the pros of those investments. Now I will get into equity securities. When it comes to equity securities there are two major types that are usually discussed: *preferred* and *common stocks*. Equity securities differ from debt securities in that equity securities allow ownership while debt securities represent a loan or an IOU. Stocks are purchased in a public market aptly named the stock market. People usually refer to the overall market as the stock market, but for this purpose it mainly refers to a place where stocks of companies are traded. The stock market can be categorized as either an organized security exchange or an over-the-counter market. Organized security exchanges physically occupy space (a building), and financial instruments are traded on the premise. The New York Stock Exchange (NYSE) and the American Stock Exchange (AMEX) are two of the three main exchanges for investors and are considered organized security exchanges. You may have seen movies where people are on the floor of an exchange shouting orders and phones ringing off the hook while seeing red and green ticker tapes. This is what organized exchanges look like with less dramatization. The NYSE trades billions of shares there and in today's time it is a mixture of both markets because it allows trading on the floor and electronic trading. The over the counter (OTC) market is a network of dealers that has no listing or membership requirements; it includes all security markets except the organized exchanges. The National Association of Dealers Automated Quotations (NASDAQ) is an OTC and is the world's first electronic stock market.

Now that you have a grasp of the stock market, we can get back to the subject of preferred and common stock. Preferred stock allows shareholders to take a preferred position compared to common shareholders. What this means is that owners of preferred stock will receive their dividends before owners of common stock. If the company doesn't earn enough to pay, then neither preferred nor common stockholders get paid however, dividends for preferred stockholders will accrue and must be paid in full before any common shareholder receives dividends. Owners of preferred stock also get a preferred claim on the distribution of company assets if the firm goes bankrupt, sells, or liquidate any assets. In the event of any of the aforementioned, the order of persons to be paid are anyone holding a bond (creditors), preferred shareholders, followed by common stockholders, if anything is left. When you get to the nitty gritty of preferred stocks you learn that this is a cross between stocks and bonds. It's similar to common stocks in that you have no fixed maturity date, dividends paid on the security aren't deductible for tax purposes, and if you aren't paid dividends, it doesn't spell bankruptcy or disaster for the firm. It's like a bond in that dividends are typically a fixed amount, much like interest payments, and you don't get voting rights. These stocks are much deeper than what's presented here with features, such as convertibility or arbitrage, that's beyond the scope of this publication.

Common stock is what most people are familiar with and what's typically purchased through retirement plans or on an individual basis. A common stock merely represents equity ownership in a corporation and entitles you to a share of the company's success, usually in the form of dividends or appreciation in value. Ownership of common stock also provide you voting rights which allows you to help make decisions within the firm. This investment tends to have certain economic concepts that you should be aware of that will allow you to make sound investment decisions: supply and demand, government actions, and good ole cause and effect.

Supply and demand is the relationship between what's available and what people are willing to pay for it. People have to want what's being supplied in order for the demand to rise. This is important in stock investing because demand drives up the price due to the desire to have ownership, but the supply is limited which means someone else has to want to sell shares. If no one wants the shares of the company, then there's no demand or increase in price. Cause and effect is basically scenario building or logical thinking. Let's say that a business is failing or that its business model is outdated. Logically it doesn't make sense to go out and purchase shares in the company no matter how much you may like it. Sound familiar right? (Tulip mania, Cabbage Patch Dolls, GameStop). The last concept of government actions deals with things it controls such as credit, public security markets, and money supply. War can also impact investments in a positive or negative way. Mainly the actions of governments manifest itself through laws, taxes, or new regulations governing securities. The goal for getting you to become your own boss doesn't lie with bonds or stocks because it's hard for an individual investor to make money trying to build a diversified bond portfolio or trade single stocks. The information I'll introduce in the next few chapters are the meat and potatoes, however, the instruments presented here are great ways to diversify your holdings if you don't want to hold a lot of cash.

Earlier in chapter one I told you that there are some investments that are available to the ultra-wealthy that provide asymmetrical risk/reward or gives them big upside with little risk. The products I am about to introduce are in that realm and are available to everyday people, like you and me, who aren't outrageously wealthy. These investments include structured products, market linked certificates, annuities, and index funds. Some of these may work for everyone (index funds) while some may not (annuities). However, I'll give you the information regardless.

Structured Products

A structured product is nothing more than two or more products combined with the anticipation of achieving a particular goal. These results aren't guaranteed so the anticipation is the key to this product, much like expected return versus actual return. Structured products tend to be offered as a *package* and can be issued under a trust. A trust is a legal entity created to control the distribution of property and is discussed in *Introduction to Financial Success* as a way to protect your assets. If you want to get technical about structured products the Securities and Exchange Commission (SEC) defines this product as "securities whose cash flow characteristics depend upon one or more indices or that have embedded forwards or options or securities where an investor's investment return and the issuer's payment obligations are contingent on, or highly sensitive to, changes in the value of underlying assets, indices, interest rates, or cash flows." This is a very pedantic way of simply saying exactly what I stated at the beginning of the section: two or more products combined with the anticipation of achieving a particular goal.

There are many structured products, and they can be called by several different names depending on the user, i.e. income enhancements, buy/write, or income writing, to name a few. A buy/write is comprised of a stock that pays a dividend and a call option. Although this isn't the structured product I want to present, I think this one is interesting to know, so I want to provide an example.

Let's say that you want to find a way to produce income by investing in securities. Imagine that you had the funds to purchase 1,000 shares of DEF common stock at $25 a share with the stock paying a $1 dividend annually or $0.25 per quarter. Currently this means a 4 percent yield ($1 dividend/$25 per share). With a buy/write product, you purchase a dividend yielding stock and a call option, so obviously your next step is to write the call options. Through your platform you stumble upon a six-month call on the same stock, DEF, with a strike price of $28 that's trading at 1 ½. This is considered an out-of-the-money call option due to the fact no one is going to call the option and pay $28 per share when it's trading at $25. With this information you choose to sell or write ten calls and rake in $1500 (10 calls x 100 shares per contract x 1.5). This is a covered call and currently you've collected 18 months of dividends already. All things being equal, if at the end of the options period of six months the option expire worthless, you will have also earned $500 for owning the shares ($.50 for 2 quarters x 1000 shares). And because the options weren't called, you can repeat the process!

Collecting the premium and the dividends sounds exciting, however, this buy/write product does have some downside. If your stock rises above the $28 and gets called away, you earn $3,000. but you lose the opportunity to produce an income stream unless you purchase more stock. The $3,000 came from the difference between the strike price of $28 and the price you purchase the stock ($25) which is multiplied by the number of shares you own and have to sell (1,000). So that's $28-$25 which is $3 multiplied by 1,000 for a total of $3,000. This doesn't include the original $25,000 you spent and received back. Another downside is that if the stock goes lower than the $25 mark, your breakeven price is $23.50 meaning that if it goes lower you incur a loss. This is just an introductory example to structured products and is very simple, but it can get complicated such as buying common stock and two options. I'll conclude this example for now and introduce you to the structured product that can help you become that financially successful boss I know you can be.

The product I want to introduce you to next is a structured note. I was presented this product back in 2018 after reading Tony Robbins' *Money Master the Game*. I got curious about this product that high net worth individuals were gobbling up, so I dug a little and learned a little. A structured note is made up of a bond and some other derivative product, i.e. future or options. A derivative product is one that derives its value from another product or products. For example, a futures contract on oil gets its value for the price of oil. Many other factors may contribute to the oil futures' value, but it is still based on the price of today's oil.

The intent of a structured note is to protect the investor's capital and to outperform the bond. This note can be issued from six months up to ten years, and at the maturity of the note the issuer is supposed to pay the investor the principal originally paid plus all or some of the profit from the derivative. Tony Robbins gave another definition in his book about this product that states, "A structured note is simply a loan to a bank… typically the largest banks in the world." Accordingly, these structured notes guarantees to pay you 100 percent of your deposit or a certain percentage of the upside, less dividends. The notes by the banks can also allow you to take more risk for greater upside. I'm not familiar with those types of structured notes, so I'll give you an example of how my structured note works when purchased through a broker-dealer.

Let's say that you have a broker-dealer that acquires a bond at a discount. The bond has a face value of $10,000 but, because of the high interest rate, it is being sold for $9,000 to remain competitive. It pays you 5 percent interest and is packaged with a call option on an index, thereby giving you a structured note that's sold to you for $10,000. By doing this you get a guarantee that the investment is safe along with the possibility for greater return. The bond alone will return your $10,000 as it matures and the $1,000 goes towards purchasing the call option in the hopes of earning better returns than the bond's interest of 5 percent. In a situation like this you may not get the interest payments because of the guarantee.

Market-Linked Certificates

This product is similar to a structured note because it gives you a small, guaranteed return and if the market goes up, you get to partake in the upside. If the market drops, you get your investments back plus a small return. The added bonus with a market-linked certificate is that you get protection from the FDIC. Like a typical certificate of deposit, this product ties your money up for one or two years. You can purchase these directly from the bank or through a fiduciary advisor. By going through a bank, you'll more than likely incur several fees, but these may be lowered if you use a fiduciary.

Similar products include equity-linked notes and index-linked notes. The names may be confusing due to the term equity; however, these are actually debt instruments and not equity securities which were both mentioned earlier. These securities represent a promise to pay you, the investor, an amount that's based on some predetermined formula. They are notes that have been combined with some derivative, i.e. option, issued on a reference asset such as stock (equity-linked) or an index (index-linked). Both products were unsecured, but affected the markets in 2008, so now they should have some collateral backing.

Annuities

This is a product I wasn't sold on until I researched further. Annuities can come in various forms such as fixed, variable, immediate, or advanced life deferred. Today I will talk about one type and that's fixed indexed. In *Introduction to Financial Success,* I talked about annuities and how they may not be for everyone. That still applies here, however, this product is a way for you to create that asymmetrical risk/reward wealthy people have used and continue to use on a daily basis.

Annuities are a hybrid security and is a way you can protect your savings or convert it into lifelong income. It's a hybrid because it's both an investment and insurance rolled into one. The investment part comes into play because you give up a sum of money to an institution in the hopes that you'll get back more. This institution is usually an insurance company that puts your money into either a general account or a sub-account, depending on the type of annuity you purchase. Investments, or premiums, can range from a few thousand dollar to over a few million. The insurance part of this security comes into play when a small portion of your premium is used to purchase the guarantee. With typical fixed annuities your rate of return is guaranteed for a certain number of years, but a fixed indexed annuity can offer you the ability to create an income that you can't outlive. Basically, this is a pension-like financial product that gives you a specific monthly income that lasts as long as you live, even if you make it to 125! Annuities are all about financial principles 1-3.

A fixed indexed annuity gives you a 100 percent principal protection that's guaranteed by the insurance company, so ensure you choose a company that's been in business for centuries and has a high rating. A product is only as good as its issuer. This product has other pros that benefit you as well. You get upside protection without the downside loss meaning that if the markets go up you win, and if it goes down you win. Sounds familiar right? (Structured notes and market linked certificates) Also, your taxes are deferred unless you have a Roth IRA, which means no taxes on your returns. This product is worth considering as part of your investment strategy as a way to maintain your boss status in later years.

Index funds

This baby is designed to mimic the performance of the indices. It's a low-cost way to diversify and match the markets performance. Index funds have to be the bomb if investment great Warren Buffett gives this product high praise. I wasn't sure about this product myself until I personally tried it after speaking to someone who has owned one for years. The person I spoke with told me, as well as showed me, how index funds worked. I weighed my options after that conversation and decided to delve into index funds. I purchased my fund in July of 2020 and by the end of the year my investment had already grown 18.42 percent. Obviously, this is not the norm, but it works better for long-term investing if you allow it. You can also get a hybrid or contingent annuity that invests in a tax efficient portfolio of low-cost index funds. This is a wonderful way to get guaranteed income for the remainder of your life if you somehow run out of money in retirement.

Index funds are great investments because they have consistently outperformed actively managed funds while those same actively managed funds have failed to beat the market roughly 96 percent of the time. By investing in low-cost index funds, you get lower management fees (less than 1 percent versus 3 percent or higher for actively managed funds), there's no cash sitting idly by waiting to be invested (which incurs another fee), and the hidden costs are much lower when little trading is done.

Throughout this chapter I told you about certain investments—structured notes, market linked certificates, fixed indexed annuity, and index funds because some of you may not want to fully be your own boss and just want to retire and live comfortably. These investments can help you do that as well as spread your risk over the long term. They can also help you invest your cash by not allowing it to be idle or earning a miniscule return by sitting in a savings account. Now that we're on track, it's time to get more into how to take control and boss up by using your own retirement account.

Chapter Three:
Introduction to IRAs

―◦⌒∽⌒◦―

"Cash rules everything around me," -C.R.E.A.M "Get the
Money. Dollar, Dollar bills." -Wu-Tang

Many of you who are reading this probably own or
have owned some sort of retirement plan whether a
401(k), 403 (b), Thrift Savings Plan, or some other
plan offered by your employer or started by you. For those of
you who've never had such an account, this is the section where
I'll introduce you to a wealth building tool that can make your
boss status a real thing. The retirement account I'm referring
to is called a self-directed IRA (SDIRA). This particular IRA
has an administrator, like all other accounts, with the added
benefit of you being able to control what you want to invest
your funds in. Any type of IRA can be self-directed. This

alternative is presented as a way to boss up because you are in control instead of some account manager investing in mutual funds that can charge way too much and eat away at your total earnings.

Government programs such as Social Security shouldn't be the main source of your income when it comes to reaching retirement age, it should be a supplement to the savings you've acquired throughout the years either through a tax-deferred or tax-exempt account. How to save for your coming retirement is perhaps one of the most important, if not the most important, economic decision you face yet many don't think about this process because its intimidating and the sums required for your retirement can be large. This is something we must all make time for because no one cares about your future like you do and you only have one lifetime to get it right. I personally don't want anyone to work hard for years only to be homeless or eating canned goods every day because of insufficient retirement income. By using a self-directed IRA properly, you can avoid that fate and learn to live your best life.

I'm not dissing any type of retirement savings plan because, as I mentioned earlier, any type of IRA can be self-directed as well as some 401s. I'm for being self-directed because low inflation keeps thresholds on your retirement plans and at the time of this writing, the rate of inflation and interest rates were extremely low. What this means is that because inflation was so low in 2020, the maximum amount that you could contribute to your retirement accounts didn't change from the year before. So, as it stands you could only contribute $19,500 to your employer-sponsored 401(k) or Roth 401(k) during 2021, with the catch-up contribution being $6,500 for anyone 50 years or older. As for traditional and Roth IRAs, the amount was $6,000 with the catch-up rate being an extra $1,000 for those 50 or older for a total of $7,000.

For years people have saved or invested in their employer-sponsored plans because we all thought that if we trusted our money to the smart and talented managers of said plans then we'd achieve financial freedom more quickly than if we did it on our own. The majority of mutual funds in these plans are actively managed meaning that some manager trades stocks actively in the hopes of beating the market. This "churning" or active buying and selling of stocks incurs many fees, diminishes your returns, creates taxable events on income you may never see, and all the while, failing to beat the markets over 90% of the time. If that's the case, then who can you trust to protect you and still get you the best return for your investment? Keith Sweat said it best: NOBODY! Therefore, instead of fully entrusting your investment to someone else, it's time to take control for yourself. Those mutual funds that your investment plan puts money into are only popular and extremely funded (I'm talking trillions of dollars, ya'll) because most people are too busy to learn how to invest on their own and may believe that a mutual fund makes them diversified. You can beat a large number of mutual fund managers simply by owning an index fund that's passively managed, mimics the market, and doesn't cost as much as the actively managed guys. However, the reason for this publication is not to get you to simply mimic the market but to acquire assets that produce cash flows, lowers your risk exposure, and boss up. So far, I've talked about retirement funds and how you should consider being self-directed. Now I'll give you reasons why and show you how it compares to other IRAs.

Traditional IRAs

In traditional IRAs, your money may be partially or totally tax deductible the year it's contributed, however, any amounts withdrawn are subject to income tax in the year of withdrawal. This applies to conversions as well. Traditional IRAs and some employer sponsored retirement plans restrict the type of investments that are held in your account. This is usually limited to being able to purchase safe, low-risk investments such as stocks, bonds, or an actively managed portfolio that combines both. Stocks are considered risky with dividends being paid only when declared but are part of your retirement plan because they have proven to be good for long-term growth. Bonds are pretty low risk with low default, especially if backed by the U.S. Government. Your traditional plans also invest in mutual funds that are managed by someone

who believes they can beat the market while charging you a myriad number of fees that lowers your overall return all the while making the manager and the company richer than you. The mutual fund industry manages trillions of dollars and siphons off just as much from individual households, colleges, retirement plans, and institutional investors.

Did you know that there are more mutual funds in the U.S. than individual stocks in the market? That means that various managers can create different mutual funds with the hopes of beating the market. If you research it then you'll see that this is exactly what's being done, managers creating various funds, hyping the "good" ones, and charging high fees for short-term performance while they get richer and you get poorer. These same managers fail to beat the market over 90% of the time, yet people continue to stuff money into these retirement plans and give up control of their financial future. It's good if you do put money into an employer sponsored retirement plan or traditional IRA, but it's the fees and taxes that will hurt you in the end.

By investing in any retirement plan that purchases through a manager, your average cost for owning a mutual fund can be north of 3% per year compared to a simple index fund with fees under 1% per year. To help you get a better grasp of how fees can eat into your growth here's an example:

Let's say that a friend and I both have $100,000 to invest and we're 35 years old. We decide to invest our money into different funds. He chooses a mutual fund that produces 10% annually, while I choose an index fund that produces the same return. The difference is that his fees total 3% annually while my fees total 1%. For the purpose of this example, we both hold our funds until we are age 65 where we will compare out accounts, so we wait for 30 years and here's what our comparison looks like:

- Fund without fees: $100,000 growing at 10% annually= $1,744,940
- Jon: $100,000 growing at 10% (less 3% annual fees)= $761,226
- Carling: $100,000 growing at 10% (less 1% annual fees)= $1,326,768

In this example Jon and I started with the same return and capital yet he earned way less than I did. His annual fees reduced his total return by almost $1,000,000, meaning that his manager and the mutual fund company earned more off Jon's money than he did. To make matters worse, his plan is actively managed and mine isn't. I earned over half a million dollars more with a passive fund. Also, taxes aren't accounted for with the entire active trading his fund engaged in, but for the purpose of this example, this will not be discussed. Overall, this goes back to principle one of finance where money has time value and shows you how compounding makes a big difference and, in Jon's case, a big negative difference. Even if Jon's fund was flat or not growing, for a few years he would still lose thousands of dollars to the high fees. Basically, with these actively managed funds you put up the capital, take the risk, and they make money regardless of whatever happens. Add that to taxes for any withdrawals at retirement age, medical expenses, and inflation then my friend Jon may be eating canned goods or living out on the streets. I wouldn't allow that to happen, but this should show you why I am all for having a self-directed IRA that you can manage and control.

Before I move on to taxes in your traditional IRA and employer sponsored accounts, I'd like to stick with the subject of fees for these managed retirement plans. The majority of these mutual funds tend to have a laundry list of fees in the fine print that's written in legalese or language that makes it hard for outsiders to decipher. You can encounter fees such as 12b-1 marketing fees, purchase fees, trading costs, and more. These seemingly small fees add up over the years and, as you saw with my friend, these fees can diminish your return severely.

I won't bore you with all the various fees that can eat away at your retirement funds. Just know that all mutual funds charge fees, some higher than others, and they typically fall into several categories:

• Management fees: these go to the advisor to cover the cost of research and salaries for the analysts and managers who work on the fund.

• Distribution charges, loads, and 12b-1 fees: these fees are mainly used to compensate the fund, brokers, and financial planners who recommend the fund. 12b-1 fees are essentially a license to print money and range from .25% to 1.25%.

• Other expenses: auditing fees, legal costs, and various fees paid to the fund director fall into this category. Mutual funds are "fee factories" that enrich everyone but the account holder.

When you add all these costs together, you end up with what's called the expense ratio or the total percentage of the fund that's charged every year. This expense is the main price tag and is the number the fund wants you to pay attention to, yet these numbers don't tell you the whole story. Expenses coming off the top are good for businesses because it lowers the taxable income of the company, but it's not good for your retirement fund. These expenses that come off top lower your performance just so some manager can perform worse or on par with the market. Plus, you may not have known, but you have to pay a fee to the administrator (ranging from 1.3% to 1.5%) annually for a 40l(k) if you have it. This can make it very expensive to own a fund in a tax-free account compared to a taxable one. Imagine saving 10% or more for retirement in a tax free account only to lose close to half to fees. Crazy, right?

Taxes are another thing you have to worry about with your traditional IRA or employer sponsored retirement plan. You might not worry about taxes starting out as these accounts are typically tax-deferred, but it's something you should be considering as you plan for the future. With a tax deferred retirement plan, such as traditional IRAs or 401(k), you aren't taxed until you make withdrawals as long as you're 59 ½ or older. Your funds to a traditional IRA are tax deductible the year you contribute but subject to income tax the year it's withdrawn. This is something to think about as your tax bracket may become higher or lower at retirement and, given the way government spending has been going, I don't foresee taxes being lower. Stimulus packages and government entitlement programs have to be paid for somehow. If you aren't ready to fully control your own destiny by going self-directed, then at least consider a Roth IRA.

Roth IRA

With a Roth IRA, the money you contribute is taxed as income the same year and any gains you earn aren't taxed the year it's withdrawn. You also won't have to worry about a required minimum distribution (RMD) should you decide to wait until the age of 72 to make withdrawals, which allows money to continue to grow tax-free. With a traditional IRA you must make regular withdrawals at the age of 72 which refers to the RMD previously mentioned. If you can afford the tax bill that will come along with converting to a Roth IRA, then it makes sense to at least consider it. At the time of this writing a single person with a modified adjusted gross income (MAGI) of $125,000 can make the maximum contribution to their Roth which is $7,000 for those 50 and over and phases out at $140,000 for income. Married people who file jointly cut out between $148,000 and $208,000. You get a better outcome with a Roth because Uncle Sam doesn't get to touch your compounded interest and you can thank former Senator William V. Roth, Jr. for that. If you are considering converting from a traditional IRA or some other tax-deferred account, then there are some things you should think about over the long-term.

We know that there are two things that are certain: death and taxes. That's why you have to plan for the in-between moments, such as health care when you get older. Medicare can cover some parts of your healthcare services such as doctor visits and outpatient services under Part B. During 2021, the premium rate you paid was $148.50, however, if you did a conversion and it somehow increased your income above a certain amount then you could end up paying more. Maybe this isn't something for you to worry about now or ever. But it's good to know and have a plan for as high-income earners paid between $208 and $505 a month for Part B coverage. You also have to think about any medicine you may need because the premiums for Part D increase if your MAGI increased. A conversion could offset the costs of future premiums according to www.IRAHelp.com.

Another negative of a conversion involves Social Security benefits if this program is still around once some of us reach retirement age. With a Roth conversion, the additional income could increase federal income taxes on Social Security benefits being that up to 85 % of Social Security benefits are taxable depending on income from various sources, i.e. pensions or withdrawals. Your taxes from Social Security benefits are based on provisional income or income for the time being, and is equal to the total of half your Social Security benefits: tax exempt interest during the year and non-Social Security income that's included in your adjusted income, not including certain deductions and exclusions. So, if you were single with provisional income between $25,000 and $34,000 then up to 50% of your benefits are taxable. The same can be said for those earning between $32,000 and $44,000 and filed jointly. If you were single and make more than the threshold ($34,000) or married and surpass the threshold ($44,000), then up to 85% of your income is taxable.

You can skirt this problem simply by delaying the Social

Security benefits until after you've converted to a Roth if you haven't already converted. There are other benefits to a delayed strategy such as you receiving an 8% delayed retirement credit every year you wait past full retirement age. If you want to learn more information on Roth IRAs and conversions, then check out Section 408A of the Internal Revenue Code under Title 26.

This may all be a lot for you with talk of IRAs, employer sponsored retirement plans, taxes, and so on. Yes, the information is plentiful and may hurt your brain, but if you don't investigate it, you will continue to live a simple life of working, contributing to a retirement plan that eats away at your growth, paying taxes, paying fees, and retiring while making someone else wealthy. Or you can take this information and gain control of your finances and your life so that you can live in luxury and pleasure. It's your choice. Reading tax codes, studying accounting, and learning the financial markets can be extremely boring and dry but I can almost guarantee that once you do, it will be worth it financially. To make it fun there are games out there to help such as CASHFLOW 101 by Robert Kiyosaki and let's not forget good old Monopoly. I'm sure there are more training aids out there that makes learning interactive and fun. So, do the work and you'll earn the pay. Plus, once you know it then the knowledge can't be taken away from you like money, stocks, or other assets and people shouldn't be able to get over on you as easily if you know your investments.

No one will care more about your retirement and how you'll live more than yourself. That's why you should consider a self-directed IRA for your funds. Not even a fiduciary, which has an obligation to perform services in your best interest, cares more than you will. Many of the financial service industry personnel provide you with predesigned products that are in the best interest of the brokerage firm. A large amount of these fiduciaries are brokers under the fiduciary umbrella and get paid to sell you products and it doesn't have to be the best available one. Through a legal loophole all they have to do is provide you with a suitable product. This allows wiggle room and can be speculative. How can you define suitable? As long as the investment meets the general direction of your goals and objectives at the time it was placed, then they are free from liability. So why not control your own future? To give you a better idea of suitability, think of the Rocket Mortgage commercials with Tracy Morgan or the "just ok" commercials about cell phone coverage.

Self-Directed IRAs

As of 2021, I'm currently in my early 30s and the prominent security company when I was growing up was ADT. They promised protection and security, which stuck in my mind. That's what I think of when it comes to having a self-directed IRA: protection and security. Having a self-directed IRA allows you the power of three forces that help you achieve the greatest returns which are asset allocation, diversification, and tax efficiency or ADT. A self-directed IRA gives you the power to invest in various other assets beside stocks, bonds, and mutual funds. You can invest in assets such as limited liability companies (LLC), tax liens/deeds, precious metals, private lending, and various types of real estate such as commercial buildings, single family homes, or raw land. This isn't an exhaustive list, but you get the idea of the avenues you can use to boss up. I'll get more into some of these assets in the next chapter, but for now I want to get back to the forces that allow you to achieve those great returns that will sustain you in your golden years.

Asset allocation will be the most important investment decision you'll make because it deals with long-term investing. It's been said that this particular force means dividing your capital between different types of investments (real estate, stocks, etc.) in proportions that you decide in advance according to your goals and risk tolerance. You should also take into account your age as you don't want to allocate a large portion of your funds to riskier investments and risk lowering your capital. This is because you may not have time to recover like someone younger in their 20s and 30s while you're in your 50s and 60s. What I've learned is that just about anyone can become wealthy, but proper asset allocation is how you stay wealthy. By using proper asset allocation according to your goals, risk tolerance, and age, you'll be able to grow your capital and be diversified in various markets that aren't positively correlated or move in the same direction. For instance, you may have 30% allocated to real estate, 25% in stocks, 15% in bonds, 10% in precious metal (gold, silver, etc.), 10% in cash, and 10% allocated to short- term trading. This asset allocation has your risk spread out over different classes with some of them having a negative correlation meaning that if one goes down in value not all will go down in value, i.e. gold versus cash. This helps you boss up because the fastest way to wealth creation is to create assets that produce income to purchase more income producing assets. People always need a place to stay, businesses will need capital, governments and other entities require funds, and if the market drops in one investment you have cash to scoop up good assets at a low cost if it makes financial sense. This is what good asset allocation allows you to do. You aren't able to do this through traditional IRAs which leaves you stuck with investments that eat away at your growth and can have positive correlation where all your investments drop together. In a nutshell, asset allocation is a big picture view that requires strategic goals that are broken down into smaller, more manageable ones through diversification.

Diversification became part of good investment strategy when Nobel Prize winning economist Harry Markowitz wrote his doctoral thesis in 1953. It's been called the cornerstone of modern portfolio theory (MPT). In this paper, Markowitz stated that as an investor people should look at a portfolio's overall risk/reward ratio when most investors, at that time made their portfolios based on individual securities and its risk/reward which basically allowed a person to ignore how that security would affect the portfolio as a whole. Diversification, in its simplest form, means not putting all your eggs in one basket. When it's spoken of you'll mainly hear it when referring to the securities market, i.e. stocks, bonds, or commodities whereby you're not putting your money into just one investment vehicle, asset, class, or industry. I would caution you not to just spread your money out into different asset classes simply because you want to be diversified. A large number of people jump into an investment based on hype or do it because everyone else is doing it. This is foolhardy and one of the most detrimental bad habits you can develop. You should learn as much as you can about an investment before jumping in. This will not always ensure a solid investment, but it can minimize exposure to risk. If you do decide to engage in an investment based on hype, which I'm not advising, then ensure you're not risking significant capital and that you can recover or at least aren't affected severely if you suffer a loss.

CARLING D. COLBERT, SR.

Taxes can be devastating to your growth in the same manner that excessive fees can. If you look at the history of taxes you'll find that originally there were no taxes in America or England. People were asked to contribute, not mandated like today. The tax money back then was used to fund wars such as the Civil War (1861-1865) and the war against Napoleon (1799-1816). The 16th Amendment allowed for taxes to be permanent in America. As you may know from history books, this led to the famous Boston Tea Party and helped sparked the Revolutionary War. Taxes were initially levied against the rich and made popular because the government sold it to the poor and middle class as a way to "punish" the rich. After the two classes made taxes constitutionally legal, the government implemented taxes on all classes. This levy didn't sit well with the rich and led them to create an opportunity to bypass the rules, which then provided them an advantage over the poor and middle class. This opportunity allowed the rich to pay taxes on what they had left instead of paying taxes first like all employees and small business owners. The way the rich bypassed the rules was through the creation of corporations. You can take advantage of some tax laws to by choosing a Roth or self-directed IRA.

It's not your patriotic duty to have your taxes increased or pay more than your fair share. Anyone who wants to can arrange their affairs so that their taxes are as low as possible. If you actually look into tax codes, you will find only a few pages about paying taxes while the rest of the code deals with how you can lower taxes. Besides the previous tools, tax efficiency is one of the simplest ways to increase your return and boss up. I'm not a tax expert so I recommend talking to a professional about ways to become tax efficient with your portfolio. Being tax efficient could end up saving you 20% or more, like GEICO, in taxes and increases the power of compounding and growing your retirement fund faster. That means you should be looking at three types of taxes more closely as a self-directed investor: *ordinary income tax, short-term capital gains*, and *long-term capital gains.*

You should pay attention to ordinary income tax because starting out a large number of people may have to continue working for someone until financial freedom or boss status is achieved. This particular tax can get as high as 50% in combined federal and state taxes if you're a high-income earner. Also, high-income earners are who the increased tax laws will affect the most, not the extremely wealthy individuals you'd think. If you can get out of what Robert Kiyosaki terms the employee and small business quadrants, then you can create money and jobs through the investor and business quadrants that deal with the other two types of taxes.

In accounting there are three types of income: <u>earned</u>, <u>portfolio</u>, and <u>passive</u> income. The goal is to get you into producing more portfolio and passive income than earned income. By doing this you allow your money to work for you instead of the other way around. Portfolio and passive income can incur either short-term or long-term capital gains, depending on the timeframe you've held the investments. You'll incur short-term capital gains taxes if you sell before you've held the investment one year, and you'll be taxed at the same rate as your ordinary income tax. This can occur with portfolio income such as stocks or bonds, which can be held in your traditional IRA. Long-term capital gains tax are incurred if you hold an investment for one year and one day or more and decided to sell. The tax on the gain has been between 15%-

20% depending on tax laws and the sitting President's stance on taxes. A large number of people typically derive passive income from real estate, which I'll discuss in the next chapter as one of the ways to get in your bag and become self-made.

By being tax efficient in your finances and in your life, you'll grow your capital and the power to compound faster than if you don't make conscious decisions. To show you what I mean, let's go back to the example of me and my friend Jon. Recall that we both earned 10% on our investment before taxes and fees. After paying the 3% annual fee, Jon earned 7%, while I earned 9%. A 2% difference netted me more than half a million dollars more than Jon over 30 years. Now imagine that Jon is a high-income earner that lives in New York. Jon has a tax rate that totals 50% for state and federal income tax, so now he's left with roughly 3.5% on his investment after fees and taxes. If you go back and check the math, instead of $761,226 in his account after 30 years Jon can expect only $280,679. That's a difference of $480,547 that the government and the mutual fund earned off of Jon's $100,000 investment. This wouldn't have happened if Jon held his investment in either a Roth or self-directed IRA, which would have allowed the fund to grow tax free. Jon could have also been more tax efficient in his life by moving somewhere where the cost of living and taxes are lower such as North Carolina or my home state of Georgia. Instead of paying $4,000 a month for rent he could find an awesome home for roughly half that and invested the difference. Personally, I'm considering moving to Costa Rica for retirement. If you'd like information on places to retire that aren't costly, then *Money* magazine publishes articles about such places. You can also consider places like Alaska (very beautiful might I add) or Washington which both have no state taxes.

In this chapter I talked about traditional IRAs, Roth IRAs, and self-directed IRAs. A traditional IRA is a good way to invest because it's better than not planning for retirement, however, after you consider the possibility of higher future taxes, high fees, and the chance that your investments can be positively correlated, then a traditional IRA doesn't sound too appealing. Yes, growing your money tax-deferred is great, but looking at the long-term view, it's better to pay on a small amount now than to have the small amount grow into a large amount and lose half to taxes. Controlling your own investments may not be for everyone and if it's not then stick to a traditional IRA or employer sponsored retirement account. I'm sure that's not you or otherwise you wouldn't be reading this.

Roth IRAs allow you to be taxed now and withdraw tax free. You also won't have to worry about making required minimum distributions (RMDs) like you would with a traditional IRA. A Roth IRA is the next best option if you're not going the self-directed route, A Roth allows you to delay making withdrawals if you don't need to which lets your money grow tax-free longer. By converting from a traditional IRA to a Roth, you're able to stop Uncle Sam taking more of your hard-earned money and any interest you'll earn. There can be some negatives to this conversion such as paying taxes on the converted amount, entering a higher tax bracket, and increased premiums for Medicare depending on if you're at retirement age. If you can afford the tax bill now, it's worth considering switching so that the rest of your funds can grow tax-free. The benefits far outweigh the negatives if you're looking at the long-term.

Even a partial conversion could benefit you if you don't want to switch all of your funds. Once you reach retirement age you lose the majority, if not all, of your deductions meaning a higher taxable income for a large number of people.

If converting from a traditional IRA to a Roth IRA can give you more financial freedom, imagine what converting to a self-directed IRA (SDIRA) can do. You're given a wider range of investments and you're in control of the assets you choose instead of some administrator fund manager that's charging you an arm and a leg for managing traditional investments. Through a SDIRA you can invest in limited liability companies (LLC), precious metals, and real estate, for starters. And by using ADT- asset allocation, diversification, and tax efficiency, your returns can be greater than with traditional investments like stock, bonds, and mutual funds. Having the right mix of assets will allow you to achieve growth in almost any situation. Spreading your capital into various classes, i.e. real estate, cash, and precious metals will allow you to take advantage of one or multiple markets when the others are not doing well.

The information presented here should have you ready to be self-made and I'm sure that you have some burning questions, especially those of you who may not have large sums of money. You may be thinking "'how can I invest in real estate" or "'how can I become self- directed" these are questions I will answer in the next chapter. So, if you're ready to get self-made using investments besides stocks, bonds, and mutual fund, then it's time to turn the page.

CHAPTER FOUR:
INVESTING IS CHESS, NOT CHECKERS

———————————⟨oᏣᎦᎦᎳᎧᎧo⟩———————————

"I didn't know who to trust, wasn't hidin' the coupe. Wasn't
hidin' my bag, yeah, I didn't know what to do. Gotta get this
money, you can't let it change you. But I can't lie, all these
hunnids got a n**** feelin' brand new."
–Roddy Ricch, *Brand New*, Feed the Streets 2

As you know from the last chapter there are three forces
that allow you to achieve greater returns and offers
you protection/security: *asset allocation*, *diversification*,
and *tax efficiency*. These forces require a long-term strategic
vision that's been broken down into tactical goals that will
allow you to achieve that big picture. In this chapter you will
learn about various investments that can be utilized in a self-
directed IRA (SDIRA) to achieve growth that you can't get

with a traditional IRA. Some of these investments can vary in timeframe, such as short-term or long-term, and they vary in risk/reward. The main focus of this section will be on real estate and varying real estate product. However, I will still give you other products such as precious metals, privately held companies, and limited liability companies (LLCs). By giving you a variety of alternative assets that aren't correlated to the market, you'll benefit if other parts of your portfolio take a dip. Also, by investing in more than one asset class you'll experience diversification instead of investing in the securities market as a single asset class. While viewing the coming investments you should focus on formulating a strategy that will give you a good asset allocation to achieve your long-term financial goals. At the end of the chapter, I'll give you ways to invest with your IRA even if you may not have the funds to do so currently as well as some prohibited transactions.

I'm a big fan of real estate and the benefits that owning and controlling property can bring, so I'll start off with ways you can use your SDIRA to boss up your retirement plan. Before I dig into real estate, I want you to understand that there are other ways besides owning physical property that allows you to participate in this asset class. There may be a large number of people who think that owning real estate means dealing with people and their problems so they will not enter this particular class. Some of the ways I'll talk about allows you to engage in real estate directly and indirectly while still making money, reaping high returns, and growing your money tax-free.

First, I will start you off with some low-risk investments that will allow you to get your feet wet before moving on to other types of real estate investments. This portion of low-risk investments will be based on real estate notes, tax sales, and simply how to go about purchasing real estate through your IRA. Second, you'll be exposed to investments that can be considered higher risk such as buying businesses, LLCs, and high-risk notes or properties. And finally, I'll give you information on investing with family members.

Real Estate Investing through Your IRA

You're probably aware that people have become financially successful or self-made for years in the real estate market. Most of the time you'll notice that people have done it by holding physical property whereby rents are collected, and the person reinvested in more properties or upgraded to bigger, better properties. What's rarely been talked about, at least from my experience, are the indirect ways that people have made tons on money through real estate without owning physical property. The low-risk investments that I'll discuss deal with real estate but not the actual holding of property, unless the worst of the situation happens and even that can be good for you as an investor.

For those of you, like myself, who love the idea of ownership, it's possible to purchase real estate through your SDIRA. No, you can't buy it and live in it now, but you can buy the home now, rent it out, and retire to that house when the time comes. Your purchase isn't limited to a single-family home; you can also purchase commercial buildings, raw land, condominiums, or mobile homes as well. I'll get more into this later, but before you decide to purchase real estate or any asset through your SDIRA you should find out if your administrator deals with those specific types of investments and if they are knowledgeable on those investments. My research was limited in this area; however, I did find one company that deals with handling self-directed accounts; this company is called American IRA. I'm not advocating the company in any form or fashion. I'm simply stating that this may be a good spot to start if you're interested in learning more on SDIRAs and assets that the company specializes in.

The first real estate investment will deal with notes. There are qualified retirement plans out there that have used notes and received good returns, which means you can do the same with your SDIRA. A note, or promissory note, is a legal document that obligates the borrower to repay the mortgage loan at a stated interest rate for a specific period of time. It's no different than any other structured loan, i.e. car loan. These real estate loans are known to come in two parts: the note itself and the security instrument (a mortgage or a deed of trust). Most mortgages are typically held by government agencies (Fannie Mae, Ginnie Mae, or Freddie Mac) and banks. We should at least know by now that any mortgage not paid by the borrower becomes a defaulted mortgage or a nonperforming note similar to several missed credit card payments. When this happens the banks have to mark down the value of the note because of federal regulations, which creates an opportunity for savvy investors. These notes can be purchased from various sources: brokers, resellers, banks, or from the person holding the note.

Notes are listed here under low-risk investments due to their security. The person who borrowed the funds for a mortgage gave an obligation stating they would pay the lender a certain amount of money on a monthly basis. If the borrower fails to meet that obligation, then you have the right to foreclose on the property. This is bad news for the borrower because they will end up losing any equity in the property, take a major hit to their credit, and possibly trigger a taxable event with the IRS. The latter may happen due to the IRS looking at the relief of the debt as the person receiving cash in hand. The person will essentially be taxed on phantom income, and who wants to pay taxes on money they never received? As an investor you would win regardless if the note was paid or not. This pertains to buying defaulted notes; however, you can purchase notes that are performing at a discount.

If you decide that you want to purchase defaulted notes, then you should consider working with reputable sellers only. There will be some extremely enticing deals out there and I encourage you not to let greed get the best of you and go about chasing high return. You should still choose to work with established dealers in the game, at least until you have a better feel for the game. Also, before you start any negotiations for purchasing notes you need to find out who you'll be dealing with whether it's a middleman, broker, or a seller. This will allow you to know if the person is the actual owner or not.

To begin purchasing defaulted notes, you'll need to first find a list of mortgages for sale. In order to do so you need to give up basic information about yourself and the type(s) of notes that you're in the market for. You may also have to sign a nondisclosure agreement (NDA) in the process. Once you're qualified as a buyer then you can tell the seller what you're looking for in the notes, i.e. defaulted, performing, first-priority, and so on. By giving up this information the seller can generate and send you a list of notes that are available for purchase. You can think of this list like you would a credit report because of the information it will provide. The list usually contains information such as:

- Current balance due

- Date of last payment
- Priority of the loan, i.e. first or second mortgage
- Property address
- Type of property, i.e. commercial, multifamily, single family, etc.
- Whether building is owner occupied, leased, or vacant

You'll have to conduct research with this investment just as you would with individual stocks or anything you're considering purchasing. For defaulted notes, it's best to determine the as-is value of the property. You don't want to overpay for the note and possibly the property if that becomes necessary. Real estate investors know that you make your money before the deal is complete, not after. That's why you should check with a Realtor who can provide a Broker's Price Opinion, or BPO, as to the property's value. If that's not an option for you, then you can use sites such as Redfin, Zillow, or Trulio as places to glean information. I caution you to be skeptical about the information that you'll see because it may not all be true. If you can, it's best to visit the property and talk with a local broker who knows the area. When establishing the estimated value of the property you should at least account for the current condition of the property and any repairs/improvements. Of course, you will not have an accurate estimate being that you may not have access to inspect the property. Buying defaulted property is essentially doing a fix-and-flip style property, so with that being said you should give yourself some added room for unexpected repairs.

The aforementioned is the worst-case scenario when buying defaulted notes. You can buy defaulted notes and mortgages that are already in foreclosure or in the process of foreclosure. By buying the note you are becoming the bank and can restructure the loan process so that the current owner can make payments, or you can foreclose on the property, however, this can be very slow and expensive. You can probably get the best deals on properties that are underwater, have a loan value that exceeds the property value, or from a property that's been in default for years.

The list that you'll get from the seller should include information as to the priority of the loan. This is important information to know once you establish the as-is value of the property. The priority of any lien or other mortgages will need to be factored into the price you're willing to pay as well. You need to know if there are any open tax liens, which is likely given the mortgage isn't up-to-date, or if the mortgage has been in default for years. You'll also need to pay off the lien(s), especially the ones dealing with taxes, which is another great real estate investment that will be discussed later. To better understand this, imagine that the as-is value of the property is $100,000 and there's a tax lien of $10,000. Accounting for the lien this now lowers the property value to $90,000 because you will have to pay the $10,000 to break even. When buying notes such as this the seller should advise you as to the position of the note, i.e. first priority or something lower.

After you complete this portion you can now begin negotiations. When dealing with resellers you tend to deal with large companies that have bought notes in bulk packages. These companies will try to get the best price they can, especially if the note is a first priority or one that's reperforming (debtor has made or is currently making payments). You'll have to make a case for your price just as you would if you were purchasing a used car. No one should pay full price for anything and by negotiating you have a chance to compare notes and possibly come to an agreement. Negotiations shouldn't be looked at as a way to game someone but as a way to ensure you are paying a fair price. In chapter one I mentioned that we tend to overestimate the value of something and with real estate it's no different, so keep that in mind when you're negotiating. If you can come to an agreement, then ensure that you have all the proper documentation that will allow you to conduct business, whether that's foreclosing on the property or restructuring the note to allow the debtor a chance to "cure" the loan.

Defaulted notes can be a great way to either participate directly or indirectly in real estate because some real estate investors aren't interested in what could amount to a distressed property or they fear the unknown. Add to this the requirement that you need to be an accredited investor and you could be in a niche market. Although this could be considered a niche market, you'll still have things that can go wrong. People tend to value things differently, so one problem you may run into is getting a proper valuation of the property. This includes getting an estimate of any necessary repairs, liens, or anything that could reduce the value of the property. Add to this what could be a long foreclosure process, and this could end up a major cash drain. Check your local foreclosure laws to find out the proper procedures. You could possibly avoid this with a little creativity such as restructuring the note to a longer term with lower payments or offering the person cash for their keys. Like I learned in *7 Habits of Highly Effective People,* you have to look for win-win situations and both of these options can be less expensive than going through the foreclosure process.

Buying defaulted notes aren't all bad news. These investments have the potential to return high profits along with the stability of not having wild market swings like stocks. Plus, you are diversified against other asset classes with the security of a first-priority note. If the idea of getting into purchasing notes appeal to you then check out sites such as www.notesdirect.com or www.noteschool.com.

Maybe you're just not that into purchasing defaulted notes. If that's the case, you can always purchase performing notes from the same sites. Performing notes are different from defaulted notes in that a performing note is not in default. Also, with a performing note most investors are looking to acquire a secure income stream, at a discount, while investors who purchase defaulted notes are typically looking for capital gains. It may be easier to think of these notes in the sense of holding actual properties whereby defaulted notes are equivalent to flipping properties and performing notes are like long-term holds. Being that both investments are notes of varying kinds, you can also find and buy performing notes from the same sources as you would defaulted notes, i.e. brokers, resellers, etc. The process is similar for both, so I will not waste your time repeating previously discussed information. Now let's move on to more important information on notes, which is valuing them.

So far all we know is that a note is a legal document that obligates the borrower to repay the mortgage loan at a stated rate of interest for a specific period of time. I mentioned how each part, principal, rate, and time can affect value in *Introduction to Financial Success* when I discuss real estate, but for the purpose of this publication it bears repeating so that you can better understand the investment product. Also, a person's creditworthiness can affect the value of a note. Now let's get into each portion that affects the note beginning with the amount to be repaid.

Taking the amount that will be repaid into consideration to the value of the property lets you know the loan to value (LTV) ratio. This allows you to decide if you want to take on the note or not given the LTV. If a note has a low LTV, or a small amount of money borrowed compared to the property's value, then it's more desirable than a loan with a high LTV. Imagine that you found the previously mentioned property worth $100,000 and you had a choice of it having a loan of either $20,000 or $60,000. Which one would you feel better about purchasing? The loan of $20,000, or 20% LTV, means that in the event you somehow had to foreclose on the property there's $80,000 in equity in it versus the $60,000 loan (60% LTV) that has only $40,000 equity. The 20% LTV is more secure and gives the borrower a higher incentive to pay.

The interest rate can be simple or compounding depending on the type of loan. Simple interest is the type usually charged on a personal loan and is interest that's paid only on the principal amount (the amount borrowed). To see how simple interest works let's say that you loaned a friend $500 for one year and charged her 2% interest. After the year is over, she'll owe you the $500 plus $10 in interest for a total of $510. Compound interest, mainly charged by the banks, is interest paid on the principal and any interest accumulated in prior periods. It's the type of interest that can make you wealthy as an investor or keep you poor as a consumer. I'll use the same example to show you how it works, but instead of 2% for a year the interest compounds daily at 2% for a year. So, on the first day your friend will owe you $510, on the second day she owes $520.20, $530.60 on the third day, and so on. Both types of interest are calculated on an annual basis and are crucial because the higher the interest rate the more valuable the note is, as well as the type of interest charged.

The term of the loan, or the amount of time over which the note will be repaid, affects the loan. This goes back to chapter one and deals with principle one where money has time value. I'm the type of person who would rather have money back sooner rather than later because even though a longer term gives you a steady income stream, the roughly 2-3 percent inflation rate eats away at the income annually. That means that I'm earning cheaper income streams annually if discounted for inflation. What you need to know about the term of the loan is that the shorter the term the more valuable the note.

Credit and credit rating can affect us in more ways than we know. A low credit rating can affect the rate of interest you pay on a loan, the price you pay for car insurance coverage, the type of job or position you can hold, and for the purpose of this investment it can affect the value of the note whether it's an existing note or one you created for a borrower. When you create a note, you become the bank and can get access to information such as a person's income, employment, and credit score. Candidates with good standings in these areas are considered prime. When you purchase existing notes, on the other hand, you're not able to get this information or the originator of the loan may not share this information with you. A word of caution: even though you're not looking to buy the underlying property, in most cases, you should still conduct a thorough investigation into the property. In particular, a title search and obtaining title insurance for added protection. Now let's get more into notes, but this time you'll be the one creating them.

I'm all for becoming the bank because you get to set the guidelines, create an income stream, and help someone else without charging an arm and a leg. You may be wondering how you can lend money to others; well I'll tell you. One way you can get in the game is by contacting a mortgage broker and letting them know that you have money to lend for real estate. Mortgage brokers aren't lenders, but they bring borrowers and lenders together and make loans that other lenders wouldn't. These brokers tend to have a list of lenders who are most likely private lenders (you). All you need to do is give one a call, introduce yourself, and describe what you want to do. By setting your own guidelines the broker will look for borrowers that seem right for you and present the opportunities when they become available. You can also approach larger real estate companies, take out ads in the newspaper, or contact your local associations that are invested in real estate letting them know that you'd like to lend money for real estate.

To show you how to be the bank and create a note, here's a simple example. Let's say that you placed an ad about money to lend in your local real estate magazine to see if you'll get a hit. For two weeks you field calls, but there are no good prospects. In the third week you finally find someone you believe is a good fit for your portfolio. You've performed a thorough check of her background—credit, employment, and assets—and you're ready to move forward. This young woman states that she's found a great deal on some raw land. The appraised value of the land is $100,000 but the seller will take $75,000 if she can close quickly. She's asking for half the appraised value, or $50,000, and she'll put up the other half. For loaning her the money she's willing to pay you 9.5% on a three-year interest-only loan. This will give you a monthly cash flow of $395.83 for three years with the original $50,000 principal due as a balloon payment, or lump sum, at the end of the three-year term. This may sound like a good deal with you collecting a total of $14,250 in interest over three years and getting your original $50,000 back, but you have to look at the situation like a bank would if you truly want to be the bank.

If you proceed with the loan as is and structure the note, you are giving up 67% LTV based on the sales price of $75,000 which is what a bank would base its loan off. The bank would have told the young lady that it will loan her 50% of the appraised value or sales value, whichever is less. In this case the sales value is less, and she would receive 50% of $75,000, or $37,500, instead of the original $50,000 she wanted. As the lender you don't want to be on the hook for 67% LTV on the property, especially raw land. It's been said that 50% is about as high as you want to go on this type of property. Therefore, you should reconsider the loan and offer this woman the 50% LTV on the property at 11.5% due to the type of investment she's making. Her payments will now give you $359.38 per month for three years for the same 50% versus $395.83 for a 67% LTV. Keep in mind that since you are the bank you can structure the loan in ways that benefit you as well such as requiring at a minimum one year's interest be paid on the loan even if the person decides to sell the property six months later. There's no need to loan out your money and get a nominal return while someone else benefits from your assistance; you can call this seasoning the loan. Notes can be purchased or created, and produce a good income stream. If you've enjoyed this real estate investment you should like these other low-risk investments as well.

Tax Sales Certificates

Whenever the owner of real estate is delinquent in paying their property taxes the county or some other taxing unit sells the right to foreclose on the property in the form of tax sales certificates. The name can be called something else depending on the state, so you may know these certificates as either a tax deed or a tax lien. A tax sales certificate can give you several rights once you purchase it. You have the right to collect lawful interest; obtain possession of the property by a court eviction; and to lease, rent, or reside in the property. With this investment you get high interest rate returns with low risk, which are pretty attractive terms to building your way to self-made status. These certificates are sold at a discount and benefit the investor and the county—it benefits the investor by allowing you to purchase a great investment below value with the possibility of owning physical property for pennies, and it benefits the county because it collects overdue taxes that can be used to benefit the citizens, as well as the county avoiding having to foreclose on the property. If you are looking to collect interest only, then there's good news because most of these certificates are redeemed. Before I get into an example, I'd like to give you a bit more information on tax deeds and liens.

I got excited when I first learned about tax liens and deeds. That's because these investments have several advantages over other forms of investments: 1) Anyone can do it. 2) They have priority over ALL other debt, and 3) There is a very small chance that you could end up owning real estate. Plus, you can earn up to double-digit interest on your investment. You should check with your individual state or whichever state you choose to invest in as to how these certificates are sold. For example, Missouri is a tax lien state while my home state of Georgia is a tax deed state. And to show you how you'll earn double digit returns, the Official Code of Georgia Annotated (OCGA) Title 48-Revenue and Taxation, Chapter 3-Tax Executions, and Chapter 4 -Tax Sales will give you important information on their tax certificates. In Georgia, if a person redeems the property by paying the overdue taxes they must pay a 20% premium for the first year or fraction of a year, and an addition 10% for every year that's passed since the sale plus redemption costs.

There's a difference between a tax lien and a tax deed. A tax lien is sold by a tax collector to help make up for any unpaid taxes on the property so that the county can use the funds for public amenities and services such as roads and schools. The definition of a tax lien is that it's an instrument that's used to secure the repayment of debt by imposing a legal claim on the collateral. This means that the government can foreclose on the property, auction it off, and get paid. A word of caution about these investments: tax liens and deeds can be more like a full-time business rather than a hobby due to long-term commitments of your time, capital, researching, and possible management of property if you foreclose. So, understand what you are willing to do if you make the commitment to this form of investing.

Through tax liens the original owner will maintain possession and ownership of the property until they redeem (pay off) the lien holder (you or the county). There may be a waiting period before you can foreclose on the property, so check with the local area of investment as to specifics. Depending on the redemption period, you'll have to pay subsequent taxes on the property until it's either redeemed or the period expires. This allows you to keep priority on the property. If you don't pay the taxes, then someone else can pay the following years taxes and wipe you out of the priority position. This brings up another important note about purchasing tax certificate. Please ensure that you're getting the property free and clear of any other liens if you have to redeem the certificate by foreclosing, otherwise you'll become responsible for those liens and any profit you'd hoped to gain could be wiped out with you in a position to be foreclosed on by another lien holder. This can potentially be avoided by having a title company do a title search.

Tax deeds, on the other hand, allow you to acquire a deed on the property rather than a lien. Deeds vary from state to state, so check with your local county or municipality to see how either version works. When dealing with tax deeds this type of investment can come in one of two forms: *redeemable* and *nonredeemable*. These forms are like night and day, so understand the type you're purchasing. A redeemable deed will give the property owner a certain amount of time to pay any taxes in arrears or they will lose the property. This is similar to a tax lien except a tax deed allows you to become the owner by virtue of the deed and foregoing a lengthy foreclosure process. Nonredeemable deeds allow you to take ownership of the property at the end of the sale of the deed. As the name states, nonredeemable deed means that there's no redemption period. With that being stated, please ensure you've done your homework on the property because you'll become liable for any and everything related to the physical real estate. Due diligence is your best friend when it comes to investing. I recommend speaking to a qualified lawyer, as well as your IRA administrator, about investing in tax liens and tax deeds.

In order to find these tax sales certificates, you can contact the county taxing authority and find out when the next sale will take place. They may tell you over the phone or direct you to the county website. For instance the website, if no changes have occurred since this writing, for Jackson County, Florida is www.jacksoncountytaxcollector.com and you'll be able to find information on property that may be in foreclosure by the time the auction takes place on a specific date. If you have a local newspaper, you may be able to find property that will be auctioned off by the county. You most likely will find counties that conduct these sales by using an Internet search engine and typing in what you're looking for, i.e. "Cobb County Georgia tax sales." Some sites may offer a plethora of properties to choose from, so you'll want to look for ones that fit your goals. You could pick out ones that are several years behind in taxes with property values that exceed the taxes in arrears if you wanted to earn cash flow with the chance to acquire a good property, or you could look for property that has been abandoned and distressed if you want to do fix and flip for capital gains. Ensure you conduct proper research or have a broker conduct the search for you. To show you what I mean, here's an example.

My friend Jon found six tax lots of five acres for a total of thirty acres. The tax rolls stated that the assessed value of each acre was $1,500, or $45,000 total. Through his research with a broker, Jon found out that each acre could go for at least $2,500. The tax owed on each lot is $1,200 for a total of $7,200. The sale of the property wasn't for another three weeks, so Jon decided to go check out the property and found it to his satisfaction. An added bonus is that these lots are in the path of progress, meaning that development and industry are moving in that direction. Because Jon wants to use his IRA, he calls up his administrator and tells her to fund an escrow account one week before the auction in the amount he wants to bid to ensure that he has the funds; this is because the taxing authority want to be paid within forty-eight hours of the sale.

The auction that Jon will be attending is based on the yield of the certificate, in this case a tax lien, and the minimum yield is 20%. What this means is that once the person who's supposed to pay the taxes becomes delinquent, they have to pay the full taxes plus the 20% interest on an annualized basis; simple interest, not compound. Think about it this way, if the county sold the lien at a 12% yield it will get the taxes owed ($1200 per lot) plus 8% interest. The other 12% (20 percent - 8 percent) will go to the buyer of the lien. So, on the day of the auction Jon waits until the property is introduced and bidding starts. There are nine other listings before this property. Once the auction on the property begins Jon offers the minimum of 20%. Someone else counters with 19%, and another person bids 17%. Jon really wants this property, so he bids 16% and gets countered with 14%. The third person doesn't counter, so now it's between my friend Jon and the second bidder. Jon makes one final effort and bids 13%. There are no counteroffers, so Jon gets the bid at 13%. This means that if the taxpayer redeems the lien Jon will get his $7200 plus 13% interest annually.

Being that this property is in the path of progress, the original owner is willing to pay the delinquent taxes. The lien is redeemed two years after Jon purchased the liens through his IRA. For Jon, this means his IRA received the principal of $14,000 along with two years worth of interest that totals $1,872. To arrive at this, you would multiply the taxes paid per year ($7,200) by the interest (13%), which gives you $936.

Now multiply that by two due to the number of years and you get $1,872. By purchasing the lien Jon's value increased from $14,400 to $16,272. Now let's imagine that the lien wasn't redeemed, and Jon was allowed to foreclose after three years. Jon would have to pay the taxes for one more year to maintain his position. Because he paid the first year's taxes, he would be allowed priority in purchasing the following years taxes. So, after three years Jon could foreclose after investing $21,600 and he would end up with property appraised at $75,000. Essentially that's triple digit annualized returns (roughly 116%) compared to the original 13% he would receive if the owner redeemed.

If the idea of tax sales certificates excites you but you don't like the idea of possibly owning property, then you may be interested in purchasing judgments. Back in chapter two I briefly mentioned judgments when discussing credit card debt and how you can convert this unsecured debt into secured debt. One of the ways was if a collections lawsuit resulted in a judgment and the other was if the judgment gets documented as a lien. A judgment is a decision by the court in a civil action stating that one person is indebted to another person. For instance, if you owned a property and the renter failed to pay rent then you could go to the courts and get a judgment against the renter. These judgments are typically secured against the person's assets. This investment can have high profit margins and can be purchased at a discount, but the major downside is you don't know *when* you'll get paid. You can contact an attorney to find out about judgments and if they are of any value; a litigation lawyer may be more preferable.

I have a good associate I met through prior military service who told me about purchasing a judgment. She told me that she was looking to grow some money she'd recently come into. A guy friend of hers told her that his dad had a lawyer that informed him about investment opportunities where he could purchase judgments and occasionally worked his way into owning the property. So, my lady friend decided she wanted to get in on the action, but only wanted to make money without owning property. Her friend introduced her to the lawyer, and he presented her with an opportunity to purchase a judgment against a local small business owner. It just so happened that this small business owner didn't incorporate or use an LLC to protect his personal assets, so he would be on the hook for the judgment amount. The judgment was for $90,000 but my friend only had $50,000, which is okay because the judgment would be a steal. The lawyer told her that was fine because judgments are usually purchased at a discount, sometimes for as little as $0.25 on the dollar. They contacted the holder of the judgment and found out that this person was ready and willing to get rid of the judgment because there was an immediate use for the funds. My friend and the lawyer talked to the holder of the judgment for a while longer and promised to call back in twenty-four hours with an offer after conferring with an accountant. The next day they called back and offered $40,000 for the judgment because they were looking for a minimum of 15% annual return for the risk if the judgment was paid in five years. The holder countered with $60,000 and was countered by the attorney with $43,000 who proceeded to explain that the holder could take money that's guaranteed now or wait and see if he would ever get paid. He also explained that his client would now be accepting the risk and needed to be properly compensated for giving up a large sum of money for a number of years that included uncertainty. Eventually the $43,000 offer was accepted, and my friend was later paid off four years later by the business owner.

You've learned about a range of low-risk investments that you can purchase through your self-directed IRA (SDIRA) such as notes in various forms, tax sales certificates, and judgments. Maybe you'll find success in these investments alone, but I would like to introduce you to one of my favorite things you can do with your SDIRA and that's purchase real estate.

Purchasing Real Estate

No investment is perfect or stays at the top forever, but I love the idea of owning and controlling real estate because a large majority of new wealth is linked to this asset class. Plus, you derive so many benefits by having it in your portfolio such as security, appreciation, depreciation, income (cash flow), tax benefits, and more. I talked about these benefits in chapter four of *Introduction to Financial Success,* but I'll mention them again.

Security in real estate means that the property won't lose all of its value like a stock could, at least according to history. The property may drop in value but most likely will never be completely worthless. *Appreciation* benefits you because it allows your property to grow in value meaning that it's worth more than what you paid for it. Imagine that home prices in your area grew at a steady 6% a year, and that you held the property for 20 years, whereby you paid $100,000 to purchase the house. By the end of 20 years your property would be worth over $300,000, or $320,713.55 to be exact. That's over $200,000 that can be tax free money, which could be used to purchase more property, make improvements, or fund retirement plans.

Depreciation has been changed and is called cost recovery by those who want to be politically correct. With depreciation, or cost recovery, you get to treat the physical structures or improvements as depreciable assets, except the land. This is all based on the useful life of the building, so for residential property the life is 27.5 years while commercial property is 39 years. So, for the same $100,000 property you'd get a little bit more than $3,600 as depreciation a year for 27.5 years.

Income is one of the reasons you should have chosen to invest through your SDIRA and it can be provided from a range of properties from single-family homes to apartment buildings. By increasing the income of the property, you can also help it appreciate in value. This can be done by raising rents, creating auxiliary income through vending machines, or making capital improvements to the property such as updating the kitchen. A higher cash flow will allow you to reach your financial goals quicker and allow you to spread that wealth into other investments.

Consult with your lawyer and accountant as to the tax benefits you can reap through real estate and how the Tax Reform Act of 1986 can help you through any passive losses that may occur if you own other properties. Real estate isn't without its flaws, which can be lowered, and can come in various forms such as negative cash flow, illiquidity, safety and personal liability, and management.

Negative cash flows occur when the monthly expenses exceed the income, which leads to covering the difference out of pocket instead of the rent(s) covering the principal, insurance, taxes, and interest or PITI. This negative cash flow could also benefit you if you own other properties that have positive cash flow through the previously mentioned tax benefits. A simple fix to a negative cash flow problem is to increase the rent or find a way to lower expenses. You could also try to create secondary income from the property by adding a washer and dryer if none are in place; leasing air space to cellphone companies; partnering with cable companies, or other creative ideas to bring in income. The illiquidity part shouldn't be a major concern when investing in real estate. You don't need to be able to convert to cash quickly like you would in the financial markets, and if you did need to sell quickly you could offer the property at a deep discount or a number of other options such as selling a portion of the equity.

Safety and personal liability can both be negated by discussing your situation with a real estate lawyer. She can help you navigate the intricacies of the real estate investment world and set up plans to lower your risk. That could mean setting up an LLC or corporation in order to protect your personal assets. Both entities will protect you in the event of something such as a slip and fall, or someone deciding to sue you. As far as management goes, you could outsource to a good management company and allow your SDIRA to collect a check.

Real estate is by far one of the safest investments around, and it has only gotten easier with the development of technology and real estate investors willing to share information. When dealing with real estate you're mainly dealing with two types: residential and commercial. Residential property includes anything that people can live is such as condominiums, apartments, or single-family homes; however, changes in the way people are living have added nonconventional housings such as tiny homes, Conex homes, and actual treehouses. Commercial property, on the other hand, deals with places where someone conducts business, i.e. warehouse, office building, or retail space. Commercial real estate tends to be cyclical in nature and can depend on the economy, major financing, and other factors. With that being said, let's get into the wide range of real estate that can be purchased through your SDIRA.

Single-Family Homes

I mentioned this earlier in the chapter, but it bears repeating here again, you can buy almost anything in your IRA, property wise, as long as you don't use it as a personal residence or place of business. The great thing about the residential real estate category is single-family homes up to a four-plex fall into this class and are all financed the same. Anything larger than four units will fall into the commercial property category and be subject to different financing rules. Investors tend to purchase residential property to generate income from rent or to take advantage of the appreciation over the period(s) held. Some investors also apply the strategy of purchasing severely distressed properties, fixing them, and selling for a profit. This type of investor is usually good with their hands or maybe work in construction; just look at the television shows and see that they usually do their own work. Property of this caliber tend to be handyman specials. To see how single-family homes can be purchased through your IRA, here's an example:

Assume you wanted to find a rental property that would produce good cash flow and came to the conclusion that single-family homes fit your investment goals. Because of the legwork that would be involved, you decided that contacting a broker would be a better use of your time. You call a local firm and tell him exactly what you're looking for, including the price range, expected income, and the class. You end the call and five days later he calls you back and gives you news he's found a property out of town in Kansas City, Kansas.

This property is in good condition and appreciates at 5.4% a year. The owner wants $150,000 for the property. Because you can't go see the property, the broker sends you the due diligence on the property and the area including the rents, taxes, and other financials. This lets you see the expenses for the property which totals $350 per month. Rent in the area is $1,400, so you do the math and realize that your annual income would be $16,800 and once you subtract the expenses of $4,200 you net $12,600. By dividing the purchase price by your net, you realize that your cash-on-cash return is 8.4%, not including any appreciation. To ensure that you're correct in your assessment you have an accountant run the numbers. She actually tells you that this is a great investment because the annual appreciation will push your return into double digits. Because of this, you immediately accept the deal and purchase the property for $150,000. Due to certain restrictions, you aren't allowed to manage the property so you find a management company that charges you 5.5% of your gross income, which lowers your net income to $11,676 per year or 7.8%. For now, your IRA gets to enjoy a nice income stream while the property appreciates and gets amortized through rent payments. You'll later benefit from the sale of the property whereby your IRA will receive a handsome payoff.

These next two residential properties are my favorite types because of the potential for increased cash flow, and the fact that you can have multiple units that lowers your vacancy rate if a person decides to move, or you have a major renovation scheduled. The types of properties that I am talking about are mobile homes and small apartment buildings.

Mobile Homes/Manufactured Homes

I grew up in the country and never really thought about how I lived on a street named Thomas Circle Road even though my maternal grandparents' last name is Thomas. In this little enclave, I had a great-uncle who owned a mobile home park, a small five or six-unit apartment, and his own convenience store with a laundromat. I admired his entrepreneurial spirit as a child and didn't fully appreciate it until I was older. To make a long story short, I have learned that mobile homes can be a great source of wealth if you apply the right strategies.

A mobile home, or manufactured home, can be defined as a residential unit that is manufactured in a factory and transported to a permanent site such as a mobile home park, individual lot, or wherever the purchaser chooses. Mobile homes are some of the most affordable forms of housing available and have only gotten better over the years. Brand new mobile homes can run anywhere from $50,000 up to six figures, but if you purchase them in used condition, you'll get them at a fraction of their original cost. I have a family member who found one for $14,000 and less than ten years old, and it only needed minor repairs. I'm talking less than $1,000 worth of repairs. I love mobile homes as investment; however, they do have some downsides compared to other forms of real estate. Mobile homes are a depreciating asset and tend to not increase in value like single-family homes or apartments. This form of investing makes up for that downside through its ability to provide you a constant source of income by the way of rent. Another downside is that you'll have to pay rent on the lot your home sits on if you don't own the land, as well as paying registration fees for tags. Lot rent can cut into your cash flow; however, lot rent can be cheaper than owning land due to the costs of purchasing and developing the land, with utilities. Mobile homes are an extensive subject being that there are various kinds as well as several subtypes. The three kinds of manufactured homes are *modular*, *HUD code*, and *RV*. The HUD code is referred to as a mobile home and are usually single-wide and double-wide; these are the types you may have seen being pulled down the highway on semi-trucks. Now let's get into an example of purchasing a mobile home and using the cash flow to grow your wealth.

This example is one that's close to home and showcases how you can profit off mobile homes even though it wasn't through a SDIRA.

I had a sibling who wanted to purchase mobile homes and rent them out so that she could build generational wealth. She found a distributor that had several for as low as $10,000 and with the cost of purchasing land and getting utilities on the property the cost would end up north of $40,000, so she decided to check with her credit union to see if there were any on their books. She contacted the asset recovery division and found out that they had several and after a discussion she found one that had an original price tag of $65,000 and was located in a mobile home park. My sister and her wife found out that the bank would accept $40,000 for the house and would even finance the purchase, if necessary. They countered with $30,000 cash if paid whereby the vice president asked $37,000. The final price negotiated was for $35,000 with $15,000 down and the remaining balance of $20,000 financed for five years at 7%. This made their monthly payments $400 a month. After asking the bank for the numbers of the property, they found out that rent in the area hadn't decreased and was holding steady at $850 per month, or $10,200 per year. The lot rent was $2,400 per year; property taxes equaled $800 per year, with insurance totaling $400 per year leaving them $6,600 annually. After paying the mortgage they would net $150 a month and after five years they would receive a full $550 a month if rent hadn't increased during that time.

Mobile homes give you another plus in that most are not on permanent foundations, so they are considered personal property and can be repossessed easily if you sold or financed a buyer. This helps you avoid having to foreclose on the buyer. In some states repossession of personal property is quick and easy, and I recommend looking into your local laws regarding this matter or speaking with a qualified attorney. Now I'll move on to small apartment units.

Small Apartments (4 units or less)

Small apartments are on the list of low-risk real estate investments due to the owner being able to finance the property as one would a single-family home. Unlike a single-family home, small apartments give you multiple units that can be rented out to help amortize the loan and generate cash flow. Small apartments are four units or less because anything over that tends to fall into the commercial real estate category and will be financed based on income from the property. Duplexes all the way up to fourplexes allows the owner to live in one of the units, hence the residential aspect, while renting the other unit(s) out. The downside to this type of property is that you cannot take depreciation on the unit you live in and may have to do your own maintenance in order to keep a positive cash flow.

I believe you comprehend how these low-risk investments work and how they can be used to provide your SDIRA a nice cash flow. The investments I have discussed here have all been considered low-risk and will help you get a feel for the market. Now I will get into some other investments that provide you a higher return with slightly more risk.

There are people out there, like myself and some of my associates, who just can't envision putting less than 100% into an endeavor. So, for those who tend to be more on the aggressive side when it comes to investing, these next few products should whet your appetite. I'll discuss buying commercial property, purchasing a business, private lending, and using LLCs. By using these investments, you can generate higher income streams for your SDIRA and achieve your financial goals quicker than if you invested only in the lower-risk options. Let's get into the nitty of these high-return investments.

Commercial Property

Commercial property can be a great investment, especially if it's already leased. Commercial property can be defined as real estate that's used by others for business purposes such as retail, office, service business, hotels, and large apartment complexes. This category of real estate can be better investments than houses because businesses can afford to pay higher rents that are based on square footage. You can include in the lease that the tenant is responsible for any upkeep to the property, which can mean less work for you. This is commonly referred to as a triple net lease whereby the tenant pays all operating costs, i.e. taxes, utilities, insurance, etc. and you receive a net rent. The downside to commercial property is that your income is based on the strength of the tenant (big box retailer versus mom-and-pop shops) or the economy. It's risky because unlike residential property if the tenant fails to pay rent, it means that the business has failed and most likely went out of business, which leaves them with no place to stay or operate. If a renter in a residential property fails to pay rent, then that person still has somewhere to live until you evict. You also need to take into consideration that larger properties may lead to larger costs in terms of any current or future repairs. Owning commercial property can be very high-risk, but with a little creativity and a good team this opportunity can bring outstanding cash flow. As of this writing, I have a friend of a friend who purchased an option on a warehouse in Atlanta during the Coronavirus pandemic and used it for music artists to shoot their music videos. This may not work in most cases so the safest bet is to find great long-term tenants to rent out your commercial property. Now let's delve into an example of purchasing commercial property.

There was a guy who had accumulated $450,000 in his retirement accounts which was converted to a self-directed IRA. He was a private military contractor who realized that he didn't want to work all his life, even though the pay was phenomenal. After some digging, he realized that real estate may be the way to go to help fund his retirement in his later years, so he contacted a broker and told her how much he had to invest and how he needed consistent cash flow and security from the property. He told her that he really didn't want to take on any debt, but if the property was an excellent match, he'd be willing to take on a small amount of debt totaling no more than $250,000. During the broker's search she was able to come up with three options that fit the clients' requirements.

The first property was a small apartment building that consisted of six units in Albany, Georgia. The asking price was $220,000 and was located in an area that was primed for growth. With the right management, the rents could be increased with tenants under contract; currently the tenants were on a monthly lease. After expenses the property gave off a cash flow of $20,000 annually.

The second property was a small commercial building in Jacksonville, Florida. The price for the building was $365,000 and has had the same tenants for a little over fifteen years. The property had four tenants that owned a dry cleaner, a beauty shop, a drug store, and a small eatery. The property generated a nice cash flow of $33,700 after expenses.

The last property was a Subway restaurant in Wichita, Kansas. The current tenant was four years into her ten-year lease and had the option to extend for two periods of five years each. The seller was asking $450,000 for a property that brought in cash flow, after expenses, of $38,500.

All of the properties seemed an excellent fit for the client, so the broker performed her due diligence on each property, which means she went over the properties with a fine-tooth comb and looked at the inner working of the property. This included a study of the financials, any legal actions, physical attributes or deficiencies, and so on. Whenever it comes to the financial structure of the property, it's best to get an accountant involved, unless you have some experience in this area, so that they can review the income and expense statement, property taxes, leases, as well as previous tax returns from the current owner. These things will allow the accountant to compile a somewhat accurate analysis for the property.

The first property showed that the client could expect a 9% annual return based on the amount invested, not including any appreciation or depreciation. The report also showed that the property was in good condition despite its age; however, this investment is risky due to the tenants being on a month-to-month lease as they are able to move out any time they want.

The commercial property in Jacksonville, Florida shows a better annual return at 9.23%. The bad part to this property is that you'll have to get work done to the roof. Also, this property shows that the current taxes are based on the last sales price which was $135,000. This means that your taxes for the property will more than double. The Subway property is the least profitable, in terms of return, with an 8.55% annual rate; however, this property comes with a triple net lease with a clause that increases rent every two years.

Once the client is given the analysis, he ponders his options. The apartment building in Georgia has a good chance for growth with the right management and the cash flow seems good. The concern with the property is the possible turnover rate of the tenants, which will reduce cash flows until long-term tenants inhabit the building. This means that this property is out of the running for him. The next property he considers is the commercial property in Florida. He sees that this property gives the best return, however, the cost to repair the roof will be a big expense with the added downside of a higher tax increase on the property. Taking that into consideration, the last property seems the most likely, even with its low return, compared to the others. This doesn't take it out of the running considering its advantages. For one, the Kansas property has a long-term lease with a national tenant. Secondly, the tenant pays all expenses so his cash flow will not be affected by any increases. Plus, the rent will increase every two years. Based on this, the client decides to make an offer on the Subway property. Because of his ability to close quickly with cash the broker submits an offer of $405,000, 10% less than the selling price, and it's accepted. Once that client found a good management company, his SDIRA received $2,860 a month. As you can see, most of the options available had risk that was higher than residential property but gave you a higher return for that risk (principle 2 of finance). For now, I'll dispense with owning physical property and discuss an option that's been mentioned before as a way to achieve higher return.

High-Risk Notes

By purchasing high-risk notes it's possible to achieve gains similar to those in the stock market. The type of notes that were previously discussed were for those in a senior position, or ones that had no other liens before them. Now you'll learn about the other types of notes that are in a lesser position and are called seconds, thirds, or so on depending on the position in the schematic of its payback. These notes are higher risk because any proceeds collected from the sale of an asset or paid by the owner goes to whomever is in the senior position first, then it trickles down to those in a junior position depending on the funds available. While it's possible to get a 10-12% return on a secured first note, you could reasonably expect 14-16% on a second position and an even greater return on lesser positions. Here's an example to get you started.

Seven years ago, I had a family friend buy a second home. The price of the house, with points rolled in, was $105,000 whereby she used $25,000 from her savings and an $80,000 loan from the Veterans Affairs (VA) office to make the purchase. This gave the $80,000 loan a senior position. To ensure all the paperwork was good, the bank used a good title company in the event the property was forfeited. If that happened the bank would get it free from any other bills.

About a year into owning the second homes a major

problem developed and needed to be remedied. There was some damage to the roof that caused it to need replacing, and that was going to run my family friend $6,000. So, she decided that she would borrow the money. She considered refinancing the first note and making it larger while using the cash out to pay for the roof. She decided against this after finding out that the interest rate would be at least 3% higher than her current rate. Her other option was to take out an independent loan on the property at a higher interest rate; however, it would only be applied to the $6,000 and not the whole $86,000. The second loan would increase her monthly payment by $120 and she didn't like either of those options, which caused her to look for another way.

During a family gathering, I overheard about her situation. I informed her that I could possibly help and that we should meet tomorrow after church to further discuss the details. The following day after church we met up at my crib. During our talk I learned that there was an $80,000 senior loan in front of me meaning that if she somehow defaulted, the bank would get the second property and I'd only get paid if the bank sold the home and funds were left to cover my note in a second position. I wasn't comfortable with that, so I had my broker look into the property more.

It turned out that the home had appreciated by $35,000 in the seven years since her owning the place. That meant that she had $54,000 in equity. You get this total by subtracting the bank loan ($80,000) and her loan ($6,000) from the purchase price of $105,000. That leaves $19,000; now you add the appreciation of $35,000 to get a total equity of $54,000. I liked the numbers so I had an attorney create a note including a clause stating that if she failed to pay on the first note it would result in a default on the second note. This basically meant that I could forestall the bank and start my own foreclosure process. Yes, I would either own the home or be required to settle the note with the bank, but once that was done there was $54,000 worth of equity waiting for me.

If my family friend doesn't default on the loan and makes her monthly payments on the notes, I still would make out good. Because of this being a risky note with a second position I gave her the loan for 15% interest. Earlier I mentioned that a second position note could command a higher interest rate than a first position note. The loan was for three years, interest only, for payments of $75 a month with a balloon payment of the $6,000 principal. That would allow $6,000 my SDIRA to grow into $8,700 in a three-year period. Imagine the rate I could have commanded if the position of my note was in a third, fourth, of fifth position. High risk notes can be great investments if you conduct your due diligence, find ways to mitigate the risk, and utilize the services of seasoned professionals who can structure the note to protect your investment.

High-risk notes will not always be as simple as the example above, so you'll have to find ways to lower that risk and protect your investment. There are several things you can do to help protect your cash, and if you have ever had credit that wasn't "grade A" then you've heard of one way, adding a cosigner. A cosigner will give strength to the borrower and holds someone else accountable in the event of a default. People don't lend their good name to just anyone, so if the borrower has someone with an excellent rating backing them your investment is more secured.

Another way to lower your risk is to get the borrower to put up more collateral. Usually, people will tend to ask for more real estate. In the example previously mentioned I could've asked my friend to tie up the equity in her first home as an incentive to pay on time if her credit was questionable. By doing this I would receive a larger return on my capital if I had to foreclose on the properties. A third way would've been to restructure the ownership of the property. By this I am inferring that my family friend could've sold a portion of the ownership to someone creditworthy, which would've allowed both people to borrow my funds. Unlike a cosigner, the person would have had an ownership interest in the property instead of simply signing as someone responsible, without collateral, if the borrower defaults.

And yet another way, which was briefly mentioned, is to pay off some of the borrowers' debt so that your note can move into a more superior position. For instance, if your note was in a third position you could have offered to pay off whatever loan is in the second position or contacted the owner of the second to see if they are willing to sell, at a discount.

Thus far I've discussed purchasing real estate such as residential homes, commercial property, or creating notes to help grow your IRA. Some of these have been low-risk investments and can help you grow your money slowly. Others have been high return with higher risk, and can help you get to your goals faster. I've already given you one way to achieve higher returns through purchasing high-risk notes, now I want to introduce you to other high return sources such as private lending; limited liability companies; and buying businesses.

Private Lending

I'm sure that most of us have "loaned" money to family members at one time or another. It may not have been a large amount, but it was still supposed to be a loan. Well, if you ever decided to lend your relatives some money for large purchases such as purchasing a home, then you may be able to help them out while still growing your IRA. No, you won't be able to loan to everyone due to certain prohibited transactions, but if it makes financial sense to do so with family members who aren't restricted then you should go for it. If you look back at the section on creating notes you'll see that you would've already entered the business of private lending. This is just an option for people like me who love family and want to help out where they can.

It's possible for you to rent your property to family members as well, however, you should avoid making a prohibited transaction and bringing the Internal Revenue Service (IRS) to your doorsteps. For your personal knowledge, there are three parts to a prohibited transaction and all three need to happen in order for a forbidden transaction. If only one or two of the elements are met, then it's not a prohibited transaction. Even though this is the case I recommend not trying to skirt the system. The three parts to a prohibited transaction are: 1) a transaction taking place as part of your IRA plan. 2) Conducting a transaction with a disqualified person, and 3) the transaction occurs between a disqualified person and your IRA plan. Keep this in mind because I'll go more into detail at the end of the chapter when discussing ways to fund investments if you don't have the funds readily available. Now I'd like to get into an example of how you can lend money to a family member.

Let's imagine that one of my sisters came to me and asked for help. The COVID-19 pandemic caused her to get laid off because of restrictions. Let's also say that she was behind on her mortgage and the bank is going to foreclose on her property. It will be a while before she can get unemployment or find a replacement job, and there's no bank willing to give her a loan at the moment because she's without work. I'm sure some of you can probably relate to this situation.

I have a feeling that my sister will find a way to get back on her feet because she's a hard worker and has a good education. I could loan her the money from my savings account to keep from losing my funds if she doesn't recover, however, I trust her with my life and consider giving her the loan even if it's considered high-risk. We've all heard that family and business doesn't mix, but to each their own.

There are several angles that I can use to make this work. For one, I could loan my sister that money via a promissory note that's secured by her property. Considering that there's equity available in the home, I'll be in a second position. Given that fact, I'd be in a secured position rather than an unsecured one if I loan the money without collateral. The downside to this is that if my sister doesn't find work, then she may have to declare bankruptcy, but I may still be able to recover if the house gets sold by the bank and funds are left over to cover other debts.

If I chose to go another route, then I could always loan her the money from my IRA as an unsecured promissory note. Yes, she will owe money to my SDIRA and only her signature will be the guarantee of repayment instead of having added security through some form of collateral, such as her house. An unsecured note will definitely put me in a bind if she declares bankruptcy because my note will be thrown into the mix with any other unsecured debt she has. I could possibly get my promissory note settled for pennies on the dollar in the best-case scenario if bankruptcy occurs. However, if you recall that back in chapter two, I mentioned that there are three ways to convert unsecured debt to secured debt which are: if the debtor owns real estate; you get a lawsuit that results in a judgment; or the judgment get documented as a lien. In this case my sister owns real estate, so I could go file for a judgment against her and her property. I most likely wouldn't go this route because to me it's just money and I can't take it with me when I die. Also, most SDIRA administrators probably wouldn't have allowed me to make an unsecured loan anyway.

<u>LLCs</u>

This is an excellent option for purchasing real estate if you lack the funds and can help you boss up. A limited liability company, or LLC, is a hybrid of a corporation and a partnership in that everyone involved purchases shares or membership interests based on available funds. An LLC is much like a corporation in that each member has limited liability and your losses are limited to the money you contributed, so you are protected from losing personal property or other assets. The good thing about an LLC is that it is not taxed twice like a corporation but instead like a partnership, unless you elect to be taxed like a corporation, where earnings are taxed only at the individual level. An LLC could be considered the ultimate investment tool for anyone looking to increase their retirement fund to a self-made boss status.

Limited liability companies have been the choice for entrepreneurs and small business owners who want to expand and still enjoy the control of investing without facing higher taxes or loss of control in an investment. So, if you can purchase real estate through a self-directed IRA why would you want to create an LLC? Well as I've already mentioned you'll get protection from personal liability; you're only taxed once, and did I mention an LLC is easily run? Plus, you'll be able to make an investment with individuals who may be disqualified if you were making an investment through your IRA. I'll talk more about this type of LLC investing later in the chapter, but for now an LLC will allow you to invest with personal funds and your IRA at the same time. LLCs in this capacity will allow you to join forces with developers who may need funds for projects such as shopping centers, commercial property, or housing developments.

Being that utilizing LLCs in this manner is considered high-risk, it's important for you to have a team that can help you navigate and mitigate the risks associated with real estate developments. At a minimum you should have an experienced real estate broker, an accountant, an attorney who deals in real estate, and a good IRA administrator who has dealt with real estate investing. An experienced real estate broker is important because they can help you find property, or properties, in which your IRA can invest. Because you're entering a different echelon of investing, an experienced broker will have knowledge and contacts that a new broker will not. Your accountant should have experience in real estate and understand the evaluation process of each potential investment. If you aren't certain what the numbers are saying, then your accountant's input will be valuable. Of course, a good real estate attorney is a must being that you'll be dealing with contracts, real estate, and not to mention the IRS and rules governing IRA investments. You'll want an attorney that will help protect your growing wealth while your other crew members continue to help you increase said wealth. Your IRA administrator will be in charge of reviewing any investments, scheduling funding, and sending the appropriate paperwork to keep the IRS at bay.

Out of all your team members I believe your attorney is the top player when forming an LLC. I say this because the attorney you choose must be well versed in contract law and real estate law. This is the person you'll have to trust to create your contracts and any agreements pertaining to the LLC, as this could affect your retirement and ultimately your life. Remember, the first rule for investing is to never lose money so that should always be the first order of business. A good attorney will include clauses that will protect your principal such as an "opt out" clause or inserting a clause that allows members who put up funds to be compensated first and those who used "sweat equity" to be paid afterwards with profits split according to the members' percentage of ownership. I learned this through a Tyler Perry show called *Sistas* where a male character, Zach, was working with a group called the Chainbreakers who worked with felons while getting them into real estate. The group contributed either hard equity (cash) or soft equity (sweat equity) in return for profit once the homes were finished and sold. I'm not an expert on all things dealing with forming and operating an LLC, which is another reason your attorney will be a top player. To show you how an LLC can work for you, let's get into an example.

Imagine that I've assembled my team and that we've been working together for some years. I've been slowly building my wealth over the years and I'm ready to move into the next level of investing because I have about a decade left before I officially retire. I contact my real estate broker and inform her that I'd like to find an investment that will give me a big payday and is secure. Using her extensive network, she goes to work to find me the investment of my dreams.

After a week of searching, she comes to me with an investment out in Houston, Texas. There's a developer that's buying up large parcels of land, subdividing them into single family lots, and reselling them to homeowners and builders. He has already used $1,000,000 of his own money to purchase the land and is in the process of trying to raise another $1,000,000 to develop the property. By his calculations he expects to realize a profit of $2,500,000 and is willing to give up some of that profit in exchange for funding. My broker conducts an analysis for the land as is and one for what it would be worth as a subdivision, and there's value in this project. To see if the numbers are good, I hit my trusty accountant up to review this project for any inaccuracies. It turns out that this is a solid venture, so I proceed further.

My accountant points out a very interesting part of this project and that's the profit margin. Much like flipping property for a quick turnaround, a project dealing with developing land can have some unknowns that can lead to added expenses, so they will need to be factored in. Based on this we conclude that it is best to see a 100% profit margin go into the project. This simply means that the profit margin must be equal to the total combined costs of buying, developing, and later marketing the property. Yes, there are developers who can operate with a smaller profit margin but it's best to protect my capital and anticipate unexpected delays, added costs, or any other problems that could occur. Plus, a 100% markup isn't that far-fetched. Actually, this project is above the mark up because it takes $2,000,000 to purchase and develop the land and there's a $2,500,000 profit; that means the project has a margin of 25% over what I desire. Now it's go time, so I hit my attorney and proceed.

A time is scheduled for us to meet with the Houston developer so that we can discuss the terms of the LLC agreement. We've already taken precaution to reduce my risk with the profit margin, but this simply serves as the cherry on top. My goal with this agreement is to minimize my risk while maximizing my profit. This example is simple because we both put up $1,000,000, so a 50/50 split is ideal. More than likely this will not be the case because I could choose to opt out at some time in the near future while the project still goes on, and the developer wants to protect his interest as well. Because we understand good business practices and we both want this project to succeed, we agree to a 40/60 split; I'll receive 40% ownership while the developer gets 60%. If this pans out, then in a couple of years I receive a return up to $1,000,000 on a $1,000,000 investment.

We've agreed on the 40/60 split, with my SDIRA owning the smaller share. The LLC agreement will reflect this and make the developer the managing partner because of his experience and expertise in the project. Plus, I couldn't manage it anyways due to certain IRA regulations. To protect my investment, my attorney had the agreement state that I'll get my $1,000,000 principal returned before the developer gets his, and any profits will be split according to the agreement (40/60). An opt-out clause was also included for two years, which is how long the project is scheduled to take. This allows me to take my profit and move on or stay if things are going well. Once the agreement is signed, I'll receive a 100% return to my IRA, or 50% a year. If something occurs that extends the project to four years, I end up with a 25% return, which is still great.

As you can see, an LLC can be an incredible investment

vehicle to build wealth. You can choose from many of these high-return investments that I've discussed thus far and create wealth quicker than you thought. Creating an LLC can build wealth, but have you ever considered buying a business? You could purchase the company you work for if it was for sale. There are several employee-owned businesses that operate around the world and if the idea of owning an existing business intrigues you, then read on.

Business Ownership

Ever since I learned that there are several restaurant chains that allow you to become a franchise owner, I've been excited. I've considered purchasing franchises such as Zaxby's, Wingstop, and Captain D's. I enjoy eating at these places and I'm positive others would enjoy having them in locations that may not be known for being convenient. I include purchasing a business in this section because it falls under purchasing real estate. If you don't believe that's the case, then you haven't heard the story of Ray Kroc and his college speaking engagement. The story claims that Ray Kroc, founder of McDonald's, asked several students what business he was in. Of course, the obvious answer a young student gave was the "hamburger" business, which was wrong. Ray Kroc told the group of students that he's in the real estate business. If you don't believe him, all you have to do is look at the locations of all McDonald's restaurants. Have you noticed that they almost always seem to be in prime locations and that the failure rate of the restaurant is almost nonexistent? Think about that for a minute. What Ray Kroc was really saying is that even if the business failed, the land on which the restaurant sat still had value and being that the land is in a prime location, it may be worth more than the restaurant alone. This can justify you purchasing a business through your SDIRA whether it's making money or not.

Businesses are most often based on cash flow and once that flow stops, then the business goes as well unless it has other assets to fall back on. With that being said, I caution you to research the investment and find you a good team to help you through your endeavors.

If you have all these other ways to grow your wealth and boss up, then why would you want to add creating or buying a business to the mix? Well, imagine that you are a computer engineer, and you took money from your IRA to create a revolutionary widget. It costs you $15,000 to start the business, and your widget sold like hotcakes. Ten years later you sold that business for tens of millions of dollars in profit that was tax-free because you used your SDIRA. Sure, you may not be able to use the money right away without incurring a penalty, but you know that you're fully funded in your retirement years and that you could fund another investment if you wanted. That's a good problem to deal with especially since we're living longer.

Buying a business shouldn't be attempted unless you have your team in place, especially if you don't know the industry the business is in. I recommend you having a team even if you know the industry or have been in that industry for decades. The team members consist of the same personnel as before with the possible addition of a broker that deals with businesses. You'll still want to consult with your attorney, accountant, administrator (IRA), and real estate broker(s). The reason I include a business broker to your team is because you are entering a new area that you or your real estate broker may not be familiar or knowledgeable with in buying businesses. A business broker can add value to your team by informing you about the business or businesses for sale. This person can also give or help determine the value of the business, recommend appropriate terms for the sale, and help you decide if the business is worth purchasing.

At its core, purchasing a business is no different than buying real estate. You still have to conduct a due diligence of the prospective purchase while ensuring that your investment is as sound as possible. Also, ownership structure is important for buying property or a business.

Remember certain structures have certain pros and cons as well as the amount of liability that you will be responsible for. To cap that off, you'll still need to ensure you're following the rules the IRS has in place for IRA investing.

There are numerous rules that govern how we can purchase as well as conduct a business within our IRA. The most important one right now is that you cannot control the business in which you are investing. This is because you are considered a disqualified person and if you controlled the business, you'd meet the criteria for a prohibited transaction: 1) you'd have a transaction that's taking place as part of your IRA plan; 2) the transaction involved a disqualified person-you; and 3) the transaction took place between a disqualified person and your IRA plan. What this means is that you shouldn't buy or own more than 49% of a business depending on the situation. This is because at last check the rule stated that you, the IRA account holder, couldn't hold a substantial interest in the corporation because such an interest would affect your judgment. You cannot be an officer (CEO, COO, CFO, etc.) of the company in which your IRA owns shares as this could result in a possible prohibited transaction even if you own less than the controlling percent of the business.

Businesses can be formed in various manners from a sole proprietorship to a corporation. Each has its own unique benefits as well as disadvantages, which is why the structure of the business is important when buying with an IRA. There are three criteria that must be met for a transaction to be prohibited: 1) a transaction must take place as part of your IRA; 2) the transaction must involve a disqualified person; and 3) the transaction must be between a disqualified person and your IRA. Taking these criteria into account, it is obvious that a sole proprietorship is out of the question simply because you cannot run the business and this structure would constitute a prohibited transaction. That's not to say that you couldn't restructure the business into forms such as a limited partnership (LP), limited liability company (LLC), or a C corporation. Before determining how to structure the business, it would be wise to speak with your attorney and accountant. This is just basic information for purchasing a business through your IRA. I'm aware that there are all these different rules and regulations in place that can cause you to wonder how you can become a boss if you are somehow hindered. Well, here's an example of how it can happen.

Imagine that a business owner approached me and asked if I'd like to invest in his textiles business. This company has a net worth of $1,500,000 and he needs $600,000 to expand his plant. The company I'm considering investing in is held as a C Corporation with the owner and his family being the only shareholders. I worked in textiles for a few years but I'm not intimate with it on the management side, so I hit up my trusty accountant so that she can do an audit and inform me whether this is a sound investment or not. As it turns out, the business is profiting roughly $210,000 a year and could make more if the company bought more equipment for use. I'm ecstatic at this point, however, I need to figure out how to best approach this.

My accountant tells me that I have two options if I use my IRA: 1) give the corporation a loan or 2) purchase shares in the corporation and become an owner. She then proceeded to give me the run-down of each option. With option one, giving the corporation a loan, I could loan the money out and ask for a 10% return which gives my account $60,000 a year in interest. That's a nice return but isn't anything compared to if the business continues to do well or increase; that's because my return would be stagnant at the $60,000. However, option two gives me an interest in the company that will grow with the company. I'd own 40% of the company ($600,000/$1.5 million = 0.40 or 40%) which would entitle me to $84,000 of the $210,000 profit (0.40 x $210,000). After her explaining all of this to me, it only makes good financial sense to purchase the shares.

Now it's a matter for my attorney to see if the structure of the corporation will allow for outside investors and determine if any changes need to be made to any documents being that the company is currently family owned and I'm looking to become a shareholder. Upon review, my attorney finds no red flags, so I'm ready to proceed with the transaction. All I have left to do after all that is to send word to my SDIRA administrator directing him what I want to do, and he will buy the shares. Soon I'm the proud owner in a textiles company that gives me $84,000 in yearly income, and as the company grows so too will my income; all of which is tax-free. Also, if

I ever decide I want to fund another project or retire, I can sell my shares and put the money back into my account.

This is merely one example of how you can buy a business through your IRA. There are a myriad number of ways to achieve this goal if you so desired. The key to buying any investment through your IRA is to conduct a thorough research and follow the rules set by the IRS. If you do that then you'll most certainly achieve your financial goals and boss up. This concludes the portion for high-return investments. Next, I will talk to you about other forms of investing that are non-real estate based which can help you build your SDIRA plan. These next three assets can provide some stability to your portfolio and even bring short-term gain and include: life settlements/ viatical, annuities, and precious metals.

Life Settlement/Viatical

If you're like I was then you probably haven't heard of this amazing opportunity before now. That's most likely because it's a tool that large banks and wealthy individuals have been using for centuries and they don't want everyone in on it. You could say that the general public has been given a sort of "red herring" to throw us off the trail to gaining real wealth. This investment is one of those that has downside protection (read: asymmetrical risk), so that your return is guaranteed. The individuals who've used this form of investing do not want to invite competition and over milk the cash cow that has sustained them for such a long time. Investing in a life settlement or viatical is relatively easy and requires no specialized knowledge or experience and is another type of asset that can be purchased at a discount with built-in equity. This allows you to buy the asset at below market value and cash out at a higher rate (buy low, sell high).

A life settlement could be defined as a life insurance contract held by someone 65 years or older who no longer wants to own their insurance plan. This can be for a variety of reasons whereby the policy is sold on the secondary market for an amount higher than the insurance company is willing the pay the insured person. These policies can usually be purchased from the seller for three to eight times the cash value that has built up in the policy. They can also be sold to an individual person or to a group of investors; the process by which a group of investors purchase life insurance policies is called fractioning. This could provide you greater diversity because the risk is spread out amongst other investors. You could look at this investment as being similar to a mutual fund except you know how the life settlement or viatical will perform, unlike the mutual fund which is subject to various factors. A life settlement is a safe investment because you're simply buying an older person out of their contract and collecting the death benefits when the time comes.

This may sound as if you're taking advantage of a person dying but you're really not. Most people have no idea that their life insurance policy can be sold, or they believe that they have only two options for their policy: continue to pay the premiums until their eventual death or surrender the policy for the cash value inside. By you purchasing the policy or a fraction of the policy through a group, you are actually providing someone with a great service and may even change their life. If someone is selling a policy the reasons can include: the person no longer needs the policy; they can't afford the premiums anymore; they may need money for more pressing needs; or there has been an update to estate laws that enabled the person to avoid certain taxes. Whatever the case is, the person selling the policy will be getting the better end of the bargain, especially if they would have received only $250,000 from the insurance company for the cash value but instead received $1,000,000 from you or an investment group.

This investment is one of the best kept secrets around and has been kept out of the reach of ordinary people. That's because in most states you have to either be a qualified or accredited investor, excluding the value of your primary residence when calculating your net worth. A qualified or accredited investor is a person having an income of $200,000 a year for at least two years ($300,000 if married) or has a net worth of $1,000,000. The required capital or at least the most reasonable requirement for this investment is $10,000 or more. Originally only large institutions were in on the life settlement cash cow, but in the late 90s the SEC decided that groups could start offering this investment to qualified investors. These groups typically make use of an irrevocable trust and have clients buy ownership in the trust. Life settlements aren't really marketed or advertised like other products because companies are usually registered as a 506 Regulation D company, which means that they make private offerings to qualified investors but aren't allowed to publicly advertise; people usually hear about this investment through word-of-mouth.

I mentioned both life settlements and viatical are ways to invest outside of real estate. Thus far I've only spoken about life settlements, and that's for a good reason. A life settlement is the term for any life insurance policy while a viatical is a type of life insurance settlement. A viatical is a life settlement where the person is terminally ill and has a limited life expectancy that's less than twenty-four months. Being that this is high risk for the insurance company and the fact that you'll be paid within a short time frame, you can expect to pay close to face value for the death benefits of the insured person. It's said that viatical gained popularity during the 80s with the rise of the AIDS/HIV epidemic. I'm for getting good assets at a discount, so that's why the focus has been on life settlements and not viatical.

Pricing of life settlements can vary because the price is based on the demand from investors. Life settlements aren't like stock or the foreign exchange where there's a listing of the prices. The price you'll pay can be based on factors such as the life expectancy of the policy holder, the amount of the death benefit, and the amount of the premiums you'll have to pay until the policy is paid or the insured person dies. For example, let's say that the death benefit of a policy you purchased is $750,000. In order to get this life settlement, you invest $200,000 and there's $150,000 expected in remaining premium payments. It also will cost you $25,000 in commissions for the acquiring of the policy; this leaves you with an expected profit of $375,000.

I feel that an expected profit of $375,000 on a $200,000 investment is outstanding with the exception of not knowing when you'll get paid. You can still make out great if you purchased a life settlement with a group because you're entitled to a percentage of the payout, i.e. you bought 10% of the contract so you're at least entitled to 10% of the payout.

Did you know that life insurance companies held and managed America's money prior to switching to 401(k)s? Yes, before we became our own source of retirement funding, people's money was saved with life insurance companies and grew safely year after year. Some of the most well-known companies offered pensions to top tier recruits and those pensions were grown and managed by you guessed it, insurance companies. If that's the case, then why aren't more companies offering pensions or switching back to having employee funds managed by insurance companies instead of some fund manager who collects fees and dwindles your account? It's because of greed and the desire to hoard the better investments for themselves and get astronomical returns.

Life settlements are safe to invest in for many reasons. One, policies are bought at a discount with a predetermined profit that's locked in. That means your return will be the same no matter what. Also, there's no need for research, economic indicators, or market fluctuations as there are in stocks. Two, life insurance companies are considered to be financially stable, especially those that are at least a century old. That's because these companies are required to maintain sufficient reserves, by each state, to cover all liabilities. If not, then the insurance company is placed into receivership and acquired by larger insurance companies. Three, the payout is from an "A-rated" life insurance company that has a negative correlation to the financial markets. Also, your money is held in an escrow account to help pay premiums until the contract matures. If the contract goes longer than the amount of premiums set aside, typically 7-8 years, then the owner(s) have to send additional money to the insurance company to keep the contract in good standings; a typical contract matures between 4-5 years.

This investment is not without its faults. Generally, there are some rules that are imposed when it comes to life settlements:

- the person must be over the age of 62 but at least 65 years old
- the policy must be matured by at least two years to avoid challenge from the insurance company

- the person owning the policy must sign a medical record release so that an assessment can be prepared
- A neutral third-party has to provide an actuarial report

The actuarial report will give an expected life of the person based on certain metrics. This can give you guidance as to whether you want to purchase the contract or not. The life expectancy of a person could be five years or twenty-five years with the only difference for your life settlement being the average return; the amount you receive will still be the same due to a contractual obligation by the insurance company. For example, say you invested $100,000 into a contract on an 82-year-old woman. If the contract has a build-in return of 48% you know that you'll receive a total of $148,000 once the contract matures. The one thing you don't know is when that will be. She may pass away in two months, two years, or twenty years. The longer the contract goes, the lower your return will be. That is why these rules are so important when you're investing in life settlements and why it's important to do a thorough check into any investment that you intend to undertake.

Banks have been paying a nominal amount on our savings accounts and certificates of deposits (CDs) while continually making huge profits every year. They have done this through Bank-Owned Life Insurance (BOLI) and life settlements. For them, BOLI is a form of permanent life insurance with the bank being the beneficiary; it's a tax shelter for them as well as a tax-free scheme to fund employee benefits. Purchasing life settlements allows the banks to bypass the collection time on BOLI and avoid fees because the insured person whom they are purchasing life settlement from have already paid the fees. Life settlements boost their profits because depending on the acquirement costs the return can range from 40% to 70% on a contractual basis. The same can be said for you if you purchased life settlements as well. Let's take a look:

Policy with a 40% Fixed Return

Maturity in Years	Invested Amount	Death Benefit	Simple Rate of Return
1	$100,000	$140,000	40%
2	$100,000	$140,000	20%
3	$100,000	$140,000	13.3%
4	$100,000	$140,000	10%
5	$100,000	$140,000	8%
6	$100,000	$140,000	6.7%
7	$100,000	$140,000	5.7%
8	$100,000	$140,000	5%

Policy with 70% Fixed Return

Maturity in Years	Invested Amount	Death Benefit	Simple Rate of Return
1	$100,000	$170,000	70%
2	$100,000	$170,000	35%
3	$100,000	$170,000	23.3%
4	$100,000	$170,000	17.5%
5	$100,000	$170,000	14%
6	$100,000	$170,000	11.7%
7	$100,000	$170,000	10%
8	$100,000	$170,000	8.75%

As you saw, life settlements can be the epitome of the saying "buy low, sell high." With a life settlement you know upfront how much you will get back in return for your investment without the wild fluctuations you'd get in the stock market. Your profit is contractually guaranteed and if you have the funds available, you could purchase multiple settlements. Add to this the high returns and relative safety similar to government bonds, and I'm practically salivating at the mouth picturing the growth of my SDIRA. Of course, there are some things that can hinder you when it comes to life settlements. The most obvious of these hindrances is fraud, which is very rampant in these trying times. I'm sure you don't want to be part of a Ponzi scheme (may he rest in peace), so the logical thing to do is to buy from "A rated" insurance companies, as well as obtaining a copy of the policy for review. Also, you don't know when you'll be paid, and this makes your capital illiquid, much like real estate. With life settlements the cost of buying can be pretty high, ranging from a few thousand to a couple of million which is why in some states you have to be an accredited/qualified investor. If you can get past these obstacles, then your IRA is on a trajectory of growth. Next, I'm going to give you another investment that's part of the insurance world: annuities.

Annuities

Annuities aren't terrible investments depending on the type you purchase, and the fees associated with them. This investment/insurance product is much like people in that they aren't created equal and there are many types. Each type will have certain benefits and drawbacks that will cause you to either like or dislike a particular annuity. To say that all annuities are the same would be like saying that "all men are dogs" or "all blondes are dumb." Neither of those stereotypes is true nor is it true that annuities are the same.

It's interesting to note that annuities date back thousands of years to the time of the Roman Empire. The citizens and soldiers of Rome were said to "pool" their money together and those that lived longer got increasing income payments while those who didn't were more than likely dead. During this, the government collected a small fee for its services. The income payments were received annually and is derived from the Latin word *annua*. Since the time of the Roman Empire annuities have basically remained the same with different variations being created.

An annuity is both a form of insurance as well as an investment; something of a hybrid (read: derivative). It's considered insurance because a portion of the premiums you pay the insurance company buys you a guarantee, which can vary according to the type of annuity. For instance, a fixed annuity grants you a guaranteed rate of return for a particular number of years while an immediate annuity guarantees income. On the other hand, an annuity is an investment because you sort of give money to a financial institution, the insurance company, with the hopes of getting back more in return. The premium you give the financial institution is placed in a general account (for fixed annuities) or a sub-account (for variable annuities). In short, a variable annuity (VA) is an insurance contract where all of the deposits get invested into mutual funds, and as I mentioned before these are fee factories. The sad part about owning a VA is that not only will you pay the fees for owning the mutual fund (3% or higher), but you'll also pay additional fees for owning the annuity. You may ask why people continue to purchase this annuity, well it's because of the guaranteed life benefits (GLB). There are multiple types of GLBs, but what it really boils down to is that most VAs guarantees that if your income goes down your beneficiary, or beneficiaries, will at least get what you originally invested.

I mentioned that annuities can come in many flavors; however, there are really only two general categories that are considered traditional: *immediate* annuities and *deferred* annuities. Annuities in and of themselves are amoral and like other forms of insurance they can either be worth the price of admission or not. The decision to purchase an annuity will ultimately depend on you and the amount of financial risk you're willing to take.

With an immediate income annuity, you're able to convert a large lump sum into a monthly, quarterly, or annual payment. This type of annuity is best suited for anyone at or beyond the retirement age who may want to convert their 401(k), IRA, or another employer sponsored plan into a nice paycheck. An immediate annuity allows you to get an income you can't outlive, and you have a concept called morality credits that benefit you as an annuity holder. Basically, an immediate annuity is insurance and it means that those who "pooled" their money together, much like the Roman citizens, will get a payout that consists of your principal, any gains, and a share of money from members who died before you and relinquished their funds. This type of annuity can guarantee that you or your significant other receives an income for as long as one of you is alive, even if you live to 120 years old. And if you're worried that you'll leave money on the table for someone else to collect and you don't want to, then you can choose an option where your heir(s) are refunded the amount you put in; however, this will lower the amount of income you'll receive and goes back to principle two of finance.

Deferred annuities entail you giving an insurance company

either a lump sum or making periodic payments over a number of years whereby your returns are reinvested into tax-deferred environments that turn into income streams when the time comes for retirement. Variable annuities are considered a type of deferred annuities. Deferred annuities have different versions with varying terms that are dictated by the issuing insurance company, and as far as I'm aware, there are three primary types of deferred annuities:

- Deferred income annuity: This annuity is commonly known as "longevity insurance" and is about making a lump sum deposit with a guaranteed income that happens later in life. It's basically for anyone who wants a safety net and fears living too long, like to 120 years old. Another name or variation of this is advanced life deferred annuity, or ALDA. This may be for anyone who has enough money in other accounts and want safety in income for later years. Typically, if you die before the payments kick in, you forfeit your initial payment; however, some insurance companies offer features such as cash refunds or death benefits to offset this.
- Contingent annuity: commonly called a "hybrid annuity" and allows you control of your capital whereby it's sent to a portfolio of low-cost index funds instead of the insurance company; however, in the event the market somehow tanks and you run out of money during retirement the insurance company will send you income until you die.
- Fixed indexed annuity (FIA): FIAs let you participate in the upside of the market, up to a percentage, without incurring losses if the market

CARLING D. COLBERT, SR.

drops. I discussed annuities and similar products back in chapter two, so fixed indexed annuities may sound familiar.

Unlike a traditional fixed annuity where you get a small, guaranteed return, a fixed-indexed annuity's growth is based on the gains of a market index such as the Standard and Poor's 500 (S&P500). If the index goes up, you get to keep a certain percentage of the gain up to what's called a "cap" or "ceiling." Take for instance how I mentioned a while back that my index fund grew by over 18%. If I had owned the index fund through a fixed-indexed annuity with a cap of 15%, then that's all I would get to keep with the remaining percentage going to the insurance company. There are some products that will allow you to keep 100% of the gains with the downside protection still in place. The catch is that the company will receive a small portion of the gains.

Fixed-indexed annuities have a slight advantage over other annuities because any gains you have are locked in and can never be lost. That means that the 15% gain I would earn on a $100,000 account gave me $15,000, so my new floor of $115,000 is the lowest my account can go. This product has its advantages as well as its fair share of negatives such as:

- You will pay a penalty for early withdrawals of you take any money out before the age of 59 ½.
- There is low liquidity, or the ability to convert to cash quickly, with surrender charges for a certain period of time if you decide to use more than 10% or more of the funds for something such as an emergency repair.
- Your growth is tax-deferred like a 401(k) or

traditional IRA, and who knows where the tax rates will end up in the future; however, this can be avoided if you use a Roth IRA or SDIRA.

A FIA can be a great addition to your portfolio depending on your needs and the stage of life you're in. Maybe other investments will set you up the way you want with no need for an annuity, or maybe you'd like to have added protection for the family just to be safe; only you can decide if an annuity is right for your circumstances. Before I move on to ways to fund your SDIRA if you have limited funds, I'd like to share my final investment which is precious metals.

Precious Metals

There are several types of metals that exist throughout the world, just look at the periodic table. Metals can be classified into two categories: *precious metals* and *base metals*. Classifications for each type of metal are based on resistance to corrosion and oxidation. Precious metals have a higher resistance to corrosion than base metals. Metals that are considered precious metals may change over the course of time, but they usually share come generic traits:

• They are traded in the commodity market
• Tend to be rare or scarce
• Available in limited quantity
• The price is reflected by the rarity or scarcity
• The metals can be or was used as currency, etc.

The precious metals I'll mention as part of investing with your IRA include gold, silver, platinum, and palladium. Platinum and palladium are precious metals from the platinum family and are rare metals that have joined silver and gold as part of the U.S. Mint coin and bullion program. As far as I know, platinum has only been a precious metal for over 400 years; I'm not exactly sure when palladium joined the fray. Precious metals may not be for you, but I mention them because central banks around the world hold gold in their reserves, and if the United States is considered a leader in gold holding why shouldn't you follow in the footsteps of the greatest nation in the world?

Adding precious metals to your investments can help create a balanced portfolio, or one that has both a positive and negative correlation amongst asset classes. In order to keep a balanced portfolio, you will have to change the allocation between asset classes from time to time, or rebalance, as one or more asset will increase more than your original allocation. Also, you may want to change your allocations based on your view of the economic future. Now let's go for the gold.

Gold

Gold has been a precious metal since ancient times. I'm talking back during the time of the Egyptians and the Aztecs. Let's not forget the famed story of Midas, who turned anything he came into contact with into gold; this story was closely based on King Croesus who was considered the ancient world's richest man. I won't give you a rundown pertaining to the history of gold, so I'll move on to more important matters.

Gold is a commodity that fluctuates on a daily basis and is typically seen as an asset of last resorts. Usually when the economy is doing well, then gold isn't and vice versa. This precious metal is prized because of its semi-indestructibility, its rarity, and its malleability. It's semi-indestructible because oxygen and heat tend to have little to no effect on it while cyanide does heavy damage. Gold is said to be one of the rarest natural resources in the world, much like its other precious metal counterparts, and tends to have various uses. Because of gold's malleability, 24 karat, or carat, gold is cherished by craftsmen; 24K gold is the purest of gold standards with lesser qualities being alloyed or mixed with other metals.

Due to the supply and demand of gold I feel it's important to understand some of the uses for gold. This may give you better insight as to why some products are priced as high as they are:

• *Electronics*: gold has the ability to conduct electricity and is ductile

• *Jewelry*: this area alone accounts for the majority of the gold that's consumed

• *Dentistry*: used in dental fixtures

• *Money*: self-explanatory

Depending on the quality of the gold that you're purchasing, this metal can be measured according to varying weights. If you choose to purchase gold through an ETF you'll find that the unit of measurement will be troy ounces (oz.). Larger quantities, such as those found in the reserves of central banks or the gold mines, are measured in metric tons. A troy ounce is roughly 31.10 grams and a metric ton is equivalent to 32,150 ounces. I have already mentioned karats or carats which is the last unit of measurement.

Gold is one of the few commodities that can be physically bought while preserving it value or increasing over time. There was a time when gold was flat at $35 an ounce, now look at the price since we left the gold standard. You can purchase gold in physical forms such as coins or bars, but to do so you need to go through dealers such as APMEX, KITCO, or find dealers by checking with the Better Business Bureau (BBB).

If you're not interested in owning physical metal you can still participate in the gold market through other means such as gold certificates, ETFs, stocks in gold companies, or futures contracts.

Participating in the gold market by owning gold certificates enables you to have gold without actually taking possession as you would if you bought through a dealer. The certificates certify that you own a certain amount of gold. By purchasing an ETF, you are purchasing ownership in various companies within the fund. They typically have lower fees, capital gains, and most importantly, you know exactly what you're getting. Plus, ETFs can be traded like stocks meaning you can day trade for quick profits. Gold ETFs will more than likely track the price of gold on the spot market, or the real time price of gold.

Yet another way to enter into the gold market is through owning stocks in companies that either mine, process, or distribute gold. I'm positive that you can find quite a few on the market, but the one that I am familiar with is Barricks Gold Corporation. This company is said to be a premier player in the gold mining business. As an added bonus to invest in gold, it tends to become popular between October and April due to Chinese New Year and the prime marriage season in India. This is because gold is a popular gift and billions of people are either looking to gift or receive gold. By the way, I'm not advocating for Barricks Gold Corp. as an investment, I'm merely providing an example of a company that issues stocks and is connected to the gold market.

With gold futures you are investing directly in gold through the futures market. A futures contract is a legally binding agreement that sets the conditions for the delivery of commodities or financial instruments at a specific time in the future. Basically, you're obligated to buy the product attached to the contract whereas with an option you have the right to buy but not a contractual obligation. Futures contracts were meant for speculators and hedgers to limit the amount of time and risk they may experience without protection. For example, if a major airline knows that fuel costs will rise in the summer but can get a contract at a lower price now, they can purchase a futures contract to buy at a lower price today for delivery in the future. These contracts are time-based and will at some point expire, and if you happen to be trading or own futures you have several options: sell the contract and take whatever profit or loss you have; sell the contract or do what's termed a "rollover;" or take delivery of the commodity or whatever product is represented by the contract. You can enter into the future market through several exchanges with each one having its own little niche. Here are some of the exchanges to look for:

• <u>Chicago Board Options Exchange (CBOE)</u>: this isn't a futures exchange per se but is mentioned because you can trade options alongside futures in a strategic manner. This is for experienced investors and should be considered with caution as you are putting more capital at risk for loss.

• <u>Chicago Mercantile Exchange (CME)/Chicago Board of Trade (CBOT)</u>: these exchanges are grouped together as the CME Group where the CBOT deals with markets such as interest rates, Dow Indexes, and metals while the CME deals with a range of instruments.

• <u>New York Mercantile Exchange</u>: this exchange trades in energy and metals.

You should be aware that there are some economic events

that can have an effect on certain markets and investments. For example, those "wonderful" stimulus packages that were part of the Biden administration in reaction to the COVID-19 pandemic caused an increase in the amount of money in circulation. The effect of this is that the money supply and inflation increased as well. As a general rule metals, oil, and agricultural products tend to rise in price when the money supply increases. A rising money supply is usually spawned by low interest rates and refers to the amount of money available to purchase services, goods, and securities. As always, I recommend that you research any investment or product you may consider investing in. Now on to another metal that makes for an attractive investment: silver.

Silver

Silver is another metal that has been a status symbol of wealth and value. It, too, has made its appearance during the ancient times. Because of silver's status as a precious metal, it acts as a hedge against inflation which was pushing 5% in June of 2021. Silver also has many applications such as industrial use, photography, and jewelry. This precious metal is more plentiful than gold and was part of the push by the Reddit group WallStreetBets to drive up the price as the group did with shares of GameStop. If you're interested in learning more about silver, you can check out The Silver Institute, which maintains a database on the market.

You can own silver in the same manner as you can gold. Typically, you'll find both metals offered together if you're purchasing physical metals through a dealer. Silver can be 99.99% pure when you buy coins or bars; however, pure silver can be mixed with other metals to create a more durable product. For instance, sterling silver is a combination of silver and copper or some other base metal such as zinc or nickel. You should probably avoid sterling silver in your portfolio as it won't provide you much value in the long-term.

When looking to invest in companies that mine silver, you should look for ones that give you direct exposure to the market and specializes in mining this particular metal, unlike gold companies who cannot give you direct exposure as a certificate or physical bars would. For all the precious metals mentioned, you can enter the markets in the same ways: physical ownership, certificates, ETFs, stocks, or futures.

Platinum

This precious metal has been called the "rich man's gold" and is one of the rarest metals in the world. It's been said that all the platinum that's been mined, it wouldn't cover the ankles if placed into an Olympic pool. Platinum is a by-product of mining for other metals and is grouped with palladium, osmium, rhodium, and a few other metals; however, for the purpose of this book I'll mention only platinum and palladium since both are currently precious metals. This metal is known for its stable chemical property, resistance to corrosion, and the fact that it doesn't oxidize when exposed to the air.

Even though platinum is extremely scarce and concentrated in a few select regions, it has been used in catalytic converters, jewelry, and for industrial use. Industrial uses include use in computer hard drives and fiber optic cables, no wonder those items are expensive. It doesn't help that this metal is one of the heaviest, weighing over twenty times more than water in comparative volume.

Palladium

As you already know from previous discussion, palladium belongs with platinum metals, and it can act as a popular alternative to platinum; it can be substituted in making catalytic converters and tends to be less expensive than platinum. Palladium can also be used in dentistry and electronics. As long as catalytic converters are made with platinum or palladium for vehicles, I think both metals will make for a good investment. There are certain companies that will give you exposure to palladium if that's what you want.

Now that I've given you ways you can invest with your IRA it's time to get to the good stuff for those of you who may not have funds immediately available to start investing in real estate. Over the next few pages, I'll give you ways to invest with limited funds and provide you information on prohibited transactions and people who you are prohibited from conducting business with through your IRA.

Buying with Limited Funds

This is what we've been building towards; it's been a long time coming. Some of you may not have a flush bank account or IRA and wasn't sure how you'd get started investing in some of the assets previously mentioned, particularly real estate. Well, I'll provide you a few ways to make those purchases, make a profit, and avoid trouble with the law. Now let's get started with good old-fashioned loans.

Loans

To my knowledge, you can borrow funds to purchase property for your IRA; however, the property in the IRA must be used as security and not the entire IRA itself. By taking this route you will create what's termed a nonrecourse loan, meaning that if the loan isn't paid back as promised the bank, or whatever lender the note was created with, can take the IRA property but can't take any action or recourse against your other assets. Little or few banks may be willing to go this route, especially if you have limited funds, so you may have to get a private loan for your IRA. This can involve some creativity and uses problem solving techniques.

For instance, you could ask the seller to act as the bank and create a promissory note to pay them back. If that doesn't work, you can ask just about anyone you know who has discretionary income or funds in their retirement fund to lend you money. It only makes sense to go this route if your IRA contributions and/or income received by your IRA allow you to make any monthly payments as you will not be able to make payments from your personal account due to prohibited transaction rules. If you find that you won't be able to make payments alone, then you can go another route.

Tenancy-in-Common

This is a possibility to consider if the cost of the investment you're considering costs more than your IRA has in it or can borrow. Tenancy-in-common ownership refers to a form where two or more people have an undivided interest in the property without the right of survivorship, meaning that if a partner dies their share will go to whomever is designated according to that person's will instead of reverting back to the other partners. In some cases, ownership is fractionalized and isn't always equal. This will give each person a percentage of the property according to their monetary contribution. A tenancy-in-common gives you and others benefits such as shares of the sale based on ownership percentage; shares of the annual income; and the ability to use your IRA and discretionary funds together for a single investment. This means that you can use money in your savings account, stock holdings, and IRA to contribute to a tenancy-in-common. Plus, family and friends can invest in real estate using their IRAs too. That leads us to our next option of creating an LLC.

Limited Liability Company (LLC)

I talked about LLC's earlier when I mentioned higher return investments. An LLC is a hybrid of a corporation and a partnership in that everyone involved purchase shares or membership interests based on available funds. Now if you want to form one with family and friends, even disqualified persons, and join forces to make investments then you can. The reason you could do this with an LLC, as well as a tenancy-in-common or limited partnership, is because you are all buying interest in the company and dealing with it or the seller, not the individual members. I recommend speaking with a qualified attorney as to the specifics as certain issues need to be addressed if you'll use funds from your IRA; and you'll need to avoid certain situations that could create a prohibited transaction.

With all this talk of investing with your IRA, the types of investments available, and the avoidance of a prohibited transaction you may be wondering how you can and cannot invest in certain situations. That's what I'll now explain in the next section.

What's prohibited and what's not?

As you now know, your IRA investments aren't just limited to traditional forms, but most people choose not to invest in other forms out of fear—fear of the unknown; fear of the IRS; and fear of success in some cases. I've learned the way around that fear of switching up your investments in your IRA, and it's that as long as the transaction isn't with a disqualified person **and** not a *specifically* prohibited transaction, then you can make the investment.

This has been mentioned before, but bears repeating: there are three parts to a prohibited transaction, and if all three are not present you don't have a prohibited transaction. The three parts to a prohibited transaction are: 1) there's a transaction taking place that involves your IRA; 2) the transaction involves a disqualified person; and 3) the transaction is between your IRA plan and a disqualified person. An LLC, tenancy-in-common, and limited partnership allow you to avoid this with the help of an attorney because your transaction takes place between the company, not other disqualified persons even though the other two elements may be met.

There is a list people that you can and cannot make an investment with if you were to conduct a transaction such as renting them a house owned by your IRA:

Those you can make IRA investments with:	Those you can't make IRA investments with:
Brothers and sisters	Yourself

Aunts, Uncles, Cousins	Spouse
Spouse's siblings	Parents: natural or adoptive
Spouse's parents and grand-parents	Natural grandparents
Stepchildren	Your child(ren)'s spouse(s)
Step-grandparents	Stockbroker or anyone providing services for your IRS. Fiduciaries of the IRA are also included along with their descendants and blood relatives.
	Children: natural and adopted

The people who you aren't allowed to invest with will create a prohibited transaction if you conduct direct business with them; however, if you happen to invest in a limited partnership and your father also invests in the business, it doesn't create a prohibited transaction.

I've mentioned several investments that are allowable through your IRA and can help grow your account by leaps and bonds. On the other side of that are investments that you cannot make with your IRA or actions that cannot be taken such as:

• Collectibles such as stamps, wine or other alcoholic beverages, antiques, and art to name a few.

• You can't borrow money from your IRA or borrow against the IRA-owned asset: however, you can make a withdrawal and roll it back into the IRA within 60 days. This can be done in any twelve-month period. If you don't roll it back into the fund, then the money will act as a loan and you'll be accessed a 10% penalty for the distribution

• Funds from your IRA can't be used to benefit you or someone else. The primary reason for your funds is to enhance your IRA. Basically, I couldn't give my sister a house loan with a rate of 3% if the market for the same loan is 8% or more

• I partially mentioned this one before, but you cannot loan funds to a business if you, a disqualified person, or a combination of those persons own 50% or more ownership in the business.

These are not all the prohibited transactions, but more of a starting point for anyone considering alternative investing that wasn't covered throughout this book.

You can do some wonderful things through your IRA, and they can either be done alone or with the help of family and friends. These types of investments happen all the time and now you can join the party. I believe in family and finding ways to create generational wealth and is one of the reasons for me putting the pen to the pad and spreading the knowledge I've acquired. Although I practice Buddhism, I grew up Christian and I recall from the book of Proverbs, Chapter 13, Verse 22 states, "A good man leaves an inheritance to his children's children, but the sinner's wealth is laid up for the righteous." Using your IRA funds, the funds of family and friends, or collaborating with others will allow you to create wealth that can extend to generations if properly planned.

I understand there's a mantra that family and business don't mix, and that's because of emotions getting in the way, misunderstandings, and greed all stopping long-term goals. Money is just a currency and a tool to invest; it's plentiful and created daily. A way around all of this is to invest through a form of business that allows everyone to reap benefits and losses based on individual monetary contributions. If everything is documented with all your I's dotted and T's crossed, then there's nothing to dispute because everyone knows what's up beforehand. I recommend outlining the details of how your investment relationship will work, who will do what, and the benefits and risks involved. If no one is down for this, then you always have other options to create wealth on your own; you can't help or please everyone.

In closing, there are a myriad number of investments that can help you boss up and get in your bag using a self-directed IRA. Investments include real estate, notes, life settlements, and a range of other investments. You're not just limited to the traditional stocks, bond, and ETFs. Investments can be low or high-risk with various rates of return. By investing in different assets, you will create diversification in the event one class declines. You never want to have your entire IRA or funds in one asset class, such as real estate, so allocating a percentage to each class before you get into the nitty gritty of investing is the strategic thing to do and it will keep your portfolio balanced if you properly manage it. Asset allocation is about strategic planning and can help you take wins and losses at the proper time while continuously growing your account. For example, you could allocate in the following ways: 30% real estate, 30% stocks, 10% bonds, 15% life settlements, 5% precious metals, 5% notes, and 5% fixed indexed annuities. I'm not saying this is what you should do, it's merely an example. When allocating your capital, you need to ensure you find ways to be efficient with taxes as they will be part of your planning if you use a tax-deferred account.

You can still use your IRA to invest even if you lack the funds by obtaining a loan and using the IRA-owned property as security and not the entire IRA. You can also do a tenancy-in-common ownership or form an LLC that will allow family, friends, or anyone with discretionary funds or IRA capital to invest. This will not create a prohibited transaction, which will occur if the following are met: there's a transaction taking place as part of your IRA plan, the transaction involves a disqualified person, and the transaction is between a disqualified person and the IRA plan. If all three are present then it's prohibited, if not then you're good. And although it may be allowed, you should consult with an attorney so that certain events will not trigger a prohibited transaction in the future.

Investing with family and friends can help everyone create wealth and enjoy life retirement years. To me, it all means nothing is you can't protect everything you've worked hard to build or pass it on without Uncle Sam taking a large percentage. That's why the next chapter is dedicated to protecting yourself and your assets.

CHAPTER FIVE:
GENERATIONAL WEALTH AND
PROTECTING IT

———◇○⟨⟩○◇———

I got 1-2-3-4-5-6-7-8 M's in my bank account" -21 Savage

This chapter is beneficial because everything up until this point means nothing if you worked hard to accumulate your fortune and you didn't create something to protect it. Asset protection can be for those of you who have children and want to pass it on, for charitable giving, to protect yourself, or all the above. Asset protection can come in various forms such as trusts, legally structured businesses, insurance, or wills. The way you structure your assets to be protected will depend on your situation, so you should consult with an accountant and an attorney on how to best proceed. During this chapter I will discuss ways to protect your assets, benefits of these methods, and how they work. I'm by no means a professional and the information contained in this chapter are only suggestions.

Wills

Almost everyone has heard of a will or a last will and testament. A will is simply a written document explaining how your assets will be distributed once you have passed away. Even though a will may not necessarily be the best way to go about protecting your assets, I still include it and think it's worth considering. If you recall in the last chapter, I mentioned that a will would decide who a partners share passed to instead of reverting back to the other partners, and that's why I'm mentioning wills here. The reason a will may not necessarily be the best method for planning is because the will has to go through probate, and this is something that you want to avoid at all costs if you have significant assets. Probate is defined as "the procedure by which a transaction alleged to be a will is judicially established as a testamentary disposition and also applies to the administration process of an estate." Basically, this means that the courts will be involved in the division of your assets, which will be costly, and almost anyone can contest the will. You shouldn't want bickering over your assets once you're gone, and with proper planning both the bickering and probate can be avoided.

I repeat, a will may not necessarily be the best method for asset protection, but it may be necessary in some cases such as designating a guardian for minor children or transferring property to a trust that wasn't transferred before your untimely demise. There are some things that will be required to make your will a legal document such as witnesses; and executor or representative; you must be of legal age; and the document must be typed or printed, just to name a few. It's important to note that laws vary from state to state, so verify the status of your will if you happen to move or change states. When executing a will, it's best to have a lawyer draft it for you, and have the lawyer safeguard it once prepared.

To create a valid and legal will, the law requires that you know the nature and extent of your property; know who'll inherit the estate in case of no will; and understand any distribution plan you've created. Upon completion of a legal will, you'll be known as the testatrix (females) or a testator (males); this will fulfill the testamentary capacity requirement for creating a legal will. As far as witnesses, you should check the technical requirements for your specific state. Most states will have similar rules such as the witnesses must see you sign and sign afterwards, or the witnesses must be competent and of sound mind. To make things easier for all parties you and your witnesses should be in the same room and use the same pen to initial or sign the documents.

Drafting a will can come in several forms and each state has certain wills that are allowed. These can include holographic wills, oral wills, statutory wills, joint wills, or video wills. A *holographic will* is a document that's written and signed by the testator or testatrix; no witnesses necessary. The downfall to this type of will is that the document can be forged, so check to see if this type of will is even allowed in your state. An *oral will* is usually accepted under special circumstances such as imminent death. Only a few states allow this form of a will and others only allow armed forces to do so before death, and then only where there's limited property. For instance, I was in the Army and deployed twice to combat. Suppose I was hit by an improvised explosive device (IED) and there was no possibility of me surviving, I could give an oral will for my personal property that I deployed with.

States such as California and Michigan allow the use of statutory wills. A *statutory will* is where you can create a legally valid will on a printed form or a fill-in-the-blank sheet. I'm not a legal expert and you may not be either, but my "spidey-senses" tell me that this could end up doing more harm than good. Saving a few dollars on the front end could cost you and your heirs on the back end. A *joint will* is self-defined and is where two people create a will together. Usually these are for married couples, and once a spouse dies the other survivor gets everything; this isn't guaranteed, however. This type of will requires steps to be taken as a contingency. And *video wills*. With the age of video recording and social media, this may soon be the way people draft wills. This type of will can be beneficial in some cases such as when memory has faded, or the person is facing imminent danger such as being trapped in a mass shooting situation. On the other hand, the downside to video wills is that the video can be altered but not as easily as a written document.

When dealing with these various types of wills, you can get so wrapped up in the creation that you forget things that can affect the will such as marriage, divorce, or children born after you've created the document. Marriage can range from getting married after the execution of a will to getting divorced and remarried. You should be aware that a large portion of states have laws that award the spouse a share of your assets, called an intestate share, unless it appears in your will that they are intentionally left out. This means that you need to ensure that you revise or make supplements to your will accordingly. In some states a divorce will void all provisions to that spouse, so you may not have to worry about making revisions; however, check with your state laws in regard to the specifics of wills. There are some states that treat the former spouse as if they are deceased, in order to protect any children in the plan, while other states the transfer of any assets to the former spouse is null and void. The only exception to this is with a life insurance policy; in this case the person who's named the beneficiary will receive compensation according to the contract and its contractual laws. This means that if you don't want that ex to get that check, then you should ensure all your records are up to date. With all this talk of marriage and divorce there may be children involved. Children come along and change everything from your daily routine to your sex life and even your will; therefore, it's wise to revise your will to reflect these necessary changes. In any case, most states have statues providing for any children born after the execution of the original will.

Even with all the precautionary measures, the aforementioned may not cover all your property. Therefore, it's extremely important to include a residuary clause within your will. This clause will provide for the distribution of the remainder of your estate after all the specifics and cash bequests have been made. It's really a blanket contingency clause or a cover your ass (CYA) clause should any other contingency or bequest you made fail for whatever reason. This is because if any of this fails, the property reverts back to the estate. Even though a will may not be the best tool to use alone, you should consider it as part of your asset protection plan. I'm sure you wouldn't want your hard-earned wealth to end up with the wrong person or have Uncle Sam benefit from your hard work. Now let's get into something that can strengthen your will.

Trusts

Trusts are the most flexible devices available when it comes to estate planning and asset protection and should be part of everyone's plan. Trusts can help satisfy different financial planning needs; it can be defined as a legal entity created to control the distribution of property. Your trust can be revocable or irrevocable meaning created during your lifetime (inter vivo) or upon death (testamentary).

Trusts are income producing entities, much like corporations and LLCs, and can be used to avoid putting substantial amounts of income producing assets into the hands of a child or someone who's financially immature. Have you heard of trust fund babies?

Throughout this book I've talked about real estate and purchasing property that produces cash flow, well a trust could be the answer to how you'll pass it on to family, friends, or charity. This form of asset protection can get complicated; therefore I recommend seeking competent legal advice. The wealthy have ways to avoid taxes and defer them legally and this is one of those ways. A trust can allow you to avoid, defer, or decrease your income and transfer taxes as well as provide control over minors and dependents through distributions.

A trust will consist of certain components that include a grantor, trustee, and the beneficiary or beneficiaries. A grantor is simply the person who creates the trust and decides what property will be transferred to the trust, who is the trustee, and how the funds may be utilized. This isn't by any means a complete list explaining the capacity of the grantor, just some basics. The trustee is appointed by the grantor and is entitled to a commission or fee for their services but doesn't receive any benefits from the trust itself unless this person is name a beneficiary. As a trustee, this person is the owner of legal title to the property in the trust and makes them responsible for the management of the trust assets, as well as keeping them separate and accounted for. If you don't appoint a successor trustee, the court will be more than happy to name one for you. The whole point of this process in asset protection is to keep outsiders, like the courts, out of your business so I recommend covering all your bases. A qualified attorney can help you out in this aspect. As far as naming a trustee, this person must be qualified to handle all financial, accounting, and management duties necessary to administer the property of the trust. The last component of a trust is the beneficiary. The beneficiary is the individual or group of individuals receiving the primary benefit from the trust property and making the primary beneficiary entitled to any income the trust may earn. Other individuals or organizations, known as remainder beneficiaries, are entitled to the principal after the entitlements to the primary ends.

Irrevocable Trusts

An irrevocable trust is one that can't be revoked or amended by the grantor. One reason to create this type of trust is for the purpose of reducing potential transfer taxes on property by removing the property from your estate. I also mention irrevocable trusts when I talked about purchasing life settlements within a group. An irrevocable trust removes the rights of the grantor to amend, revoke, or alter the trust in any way. It also removes your ability to control ownership enjoyment of the property or income generated by the property.

Inter Vivo Trusts

An inter vivo trust can be revocable or irrevocable and is made while the grantor is still alive. A trust of this kind can be made in one of two ways: the grantor can declare the holding of personal property for the benefit of another or the grantor can transfer title to a trustee for the benefit of his or herself, another person, or group of people. The first way in which to create an inter vivo trust is known as a declaration of trust and is where the grantor becomes the trustee. This could be an issue and raise questions regarding the validity of the trust. This will happen when the grantor serves as the trustee and sole beneficiary of the trust and no valid trust intent can be found. One reason that a person may create this type of trust is to take advantage of the tax benefits as it allows you to shift income from one person to another. The validity of your trust won't be questioned as long as there's an interest created for the beneficiary other than the grantor; this will still be valid even if the grantor decides to retain extensive power over the trust.

Testamentary Trust

A testamentary trust is created in accordance to your will and takes affect only after your death. Most of the time testamentary trusts are used when a person doesn't want to part with a certain property during their lifetime but wants the control that a trust provides. It's important for you to know that a trust of this kind won't result in any immediate estate or income tax savings but may do so when the will is executed.

Trusts come in various forms that can be used for just about anything. If you're like me and have children that you would like to pass wealth on to, then you should look into creating a dynasty trust. This is another form that wealthy individuals use to continuously create generational wealth for their families long after the grantor has passed. When you transfer property to a trust and take advantage of the unified credit and generational-skipping tax exemption you and your descendants could defer payments of any future tax on property for a century or more. The great thing about a dynasty trust is that it allows you to create life income interests in successive generations, and you don't have to worry about if you're currently married or on the brink of divorce because a dynasty trust will protect the beneficiary's assets from being taken in a divorce proceeding or against any creditors. Like I've said before, I am by no means a lawyer or legal expert, so consult with your attorney in regards to the specifics of a dynasty trust.

Insurance

Life insurance is something that can't be emphasized enough when it comes to planning your estate. In some cases, this may be the single largest asset a person owns. Having life insurance helps improve your estate planning for the family and develops optimum value at death unless you sell it in the form of a life settlement. Trillions of dollars in estates are waiting to be passed on to succeeding generations, and this can be both a good thing and a bad thing; good because someone made plans to keep their family going after death, but bad because of the potential transfer tax rates and any death rates that may be applied by the state. These alone can eat away at the wealth that you intended to leave behind.

This is where sufficient life insurance coverage can be helpful to your planning. There are many reasons for acquiring life insurance such as: the ability to provide liquidity to satisfy transfer taxes; you create assets in an estate; you can shelter assets against transfer tax and maximize the transfer of property; and insurance can allow you to replace income that is lost by your death if you are the primary money maker. Insurance can offer some favored tax advantages and any borrowing against the policy is usually favorable and tax-free, which can allow you to purchase assets such as real estate. As far as potential transfer taxes, you can create what's known as a life insurance trust that will pass on the insurance proceeds free of the transfer tax to beneficiaries.

You have your pick of the litter when it comes to choosing insurance policies. The types of policies include term, whole life, variable, universal life and annuities just to begin with. With term insurance you'll get the advantage of low costs. Term insurance can have many variations and isn't based on an investment element like other forms of insurance. The setback to term insurance is that as you get older it will end up costing you more to be insured under the policy. This type of insurance is typically for younger people or someone needing coverage for a short timeframe.

Whole life insurance is one of the insurance policy concepts that have an investment element to it. With whole life insurance your death benefits are fixed as well as the maturity date, premiums, and the progression of cash value. These policies are the ones usually sold as life settlements because of the cash value, especially ones with high cash value. An advantage of the whole life policy is that it allows you to borrow against the cash value for emergencies, to pay off debt, or for investing purposes. Many people have borrowed against their policies to fund or start a business, pay for a child's college, or other things. The buildup of cash can be looked at as a forced savings plan for those of you who can't seem to save. You should research this type of insurance before jumping headfirst.

Variable life insurance is simply a variation of whole life insurance that allows the flexibility in the choice of investment vehicles. You can invest your net premiums in a fund or funds of your choosing, but the downside is that if the markets fall it will have a severe effect on your policy. On the other hand, if the fund you choose earns more than a specified return your death benefit and cash value will increase with the benefit that your face value will not drop if the fund earns less. It's no different than investing, so if you know what you're doing and have done some adequate research this type of policy may be right for you; it could eventually become another form of a defined contribution plan for you.

Universal life insurance is a popular insurance policy that combines the features of a whole life and term insurance plan. This plan is flexible in the face value and premium payments where part of the premiums are invested in a cash fund that's then invested in fixed income assets. The other portion of the premiums is used to finance renewable term insurance. You can increase or decrease the amount of the death benefit as well because of the ability to vary the premium payments. Check with your insurer as to the specifics because you could end up with tax liabilities.

Life insurances are mentioned in asset protection because it is one of the first financial tools of the Western world and dates back to ancient Rome. Also, you can't purchase it through your IRA, as far as I know. Life insurance has been a source of protections and a lifeline that has stood the test of time and saved millions from financial disaster from individual people to businesses. Did you know that wealthy individuals, banks, and businesses have used life insurance as a way to build wealth? Well, it's true, and has saved or helped businesses such as McDonald's and Walt Disney.

Life insurance has been known to deal with issues such as debt, inflation, and taxes which is why it's part of the way you can protect what you've built. Also, you know that your money is safe in a life insurance policy and you can sell it on the secondary markets later if you no longer need it. Policies with cash value play a significant role for people and businesses as organizations buy life insurance and use it for a variety of reasons while increasing their financial stability, reducing tax liability, and funding your employee pension or healthcare. This is where corporate owned life insurance (COLI) or bank owned life insurance (BOLI) play a part and was mentioned earlier. Banks have billions in these policies.

Wealthy individuals have been using this secret for quite some time and their version is known as private placement life insurance or PPLI. By owning this type of life insurance, they have taken advantage of benefits such as unlimited contributions (with no income limits like certain products), no taxes on growth, no taxes for heirs, and no tax when they decide to access the money if it was structured correctly. PPLI isn't your typical life insurance policy and is an insurance wrapper that invests in a variety of funds. The great thing about PPLI is that if you ever need to access the funds in the policy you can "loan" yourself the funds instead of borrowing. A loan would be legitimate, it's not taxable, and you can repay the loan at a future date of your choosing or allow the insurance proceeds to pay the loan off after death.

The sad thing is that you must be an accredited investor and invest the minimum of $250,000 for four years with PPLI; however, you can still get similar services through a policy that mimics its nature. This is possible through TIAA-CREF, which was founded by Andrew Carnegie over a century ago. This nonprofit was for teachers only, but now offers financial services to the general public. You can visit www.tiaa-cref.org to acquire this product on your own or ask an advisor to help guide you in the setup.

Legal Structures

I saved this form of asset protection last for multiple reasons. One, if you plan properly your assets can be better protected from claims against third parties. Two, devices that are mentioned here can afford you better protections than that are above the previously mentioned insurance plans. And three, I just thought it was a fitting end for the chapter. The two structures that I'll mention are the limited liability company (LLC), which you are already familiar with, and the family limited partnership (FLP). And just for general knowledge, I'll introduce you to the other structures that may or may not offer the best protections; this will include sole-proprietorships, partnerships, and corporations.

Limited Liability Company (LLC)

This wonderful little entity offers the same limited liability as a corporation, but may be taxed as a partnership or corporation. In all actuality, it's a hybrid partnership-corporate entity. This organizational form comes from the need and desire for a structure that's taxed as a partnership yet protects its owners from unlimited liability. This business structure is fairly new with the first LLC being enacted in 1977 in the state of Wyoming. Roughly forty states or so have approved this business entity with Wyoming and Nevada (Las Vegas) being the most favorable towards LLCs.

An LLC, under most definitions, is an unincorporated structure with two or more members formed under state law. This definition fails to mention that you can also have one member LLCs. Creating an LLC is as simple as filling out the appropriate paperwork or articles of organizations and filing it with your appropriate state agency. An article of organization will state the name of the business or entity, when it was created, names of any managers, and the nature of the business. Your LLC should also have an operating agreement describing the interest of each member regarding any capital, profits, and liabilities. This is important if there's more than one member with ownership interest. There are many companies out there than can help you conduct all the paperwork if you choose not to do all of the groundwork such as Legal Zoom.

Any owners in the LLC are referred to as members and all members are responsible for the management of the LLC unless specified in the operating agreement that one or more managers should handle the affairs of the company. Creating an LLC has many advantages such as the protection of personal assets, absence of personal liability, the avoidance of double taxation, flexibility in management and organization, as well as the ability of foreign investment. The downside of this entity is that you can't issue stock and the LLC may be limited to a certain lifespan such as 30 years. LLCs are great for your asset protection plan as well as the next structure.

Family Limited Partnership (FLP)

A family limited partnership is said to be a legal entity that can provide asset protections and allows for management and control of assets; sounds a lot like a trust, right? For many wealthy families this has been, or at least can be, a cornerstone for the transfer of wealth. An FLP allows you to do business in a partnership form and limits your liability much like an LLC. If you decide to use an FLP, you will contribute property to a limited partnership in exchange for general and limited partnership interests. Afterwards, you could gift limited partnerships to family members or a trust for their benefit while you maintain the general partnership. This in effect allows you to clear the property out of your personal estate thereby reducing taxes and possibly allowing your family to take advantage of the generation-skipping transfer tax exemption. A generation-skipping tax is one that is imposed on you by the government to prevent you from passing on property to two or more generations below you without paying a transfer tax; you know Uncle Sam wants his piece of the pie. At the time of this writing the rate was between 35% and 40% of the property value that's transferred. Also, each individual that you gift to was allowed up to a $5,000,000 transfer tax exemption; it may be higher now.

This is why an FLP can be advantageous to have. Along with the potential to prevent high taxes that diminishes you family wealth, an FLP has other benefits such as you can shelter the gift from creditors of the recipient; there's reduced asset values (between 10% and 50%) for transfer tax purposes through discount valuations; you can act as the general partner and maintain control of the assets while making substantial gifts amongst other things. You can get the most advantage form an FLP by transferring property that will appreciate in value such as real estate or securities; this can be even better if you use a combination of a FLP and an asset protection trust. This can be achieved by transferring one or more gifts to the trust of a limited partners interest (your family member). Overall, you can easily protect and pass on your assets if you utilize the proper entities. I recommend consulting with an attorney as how to best protect yourself and assets regarding your situation. Next, I'll include other structures that are good for general information but may not affect your asset protection plan.

Other Forms of Business Organizations
Sole-Proprietorship

This organization is one owned by a single individual and is responsible for all business debt. There's no separation between the owner and the business and can be known as "doing business as" or DBA if you're using a name other than your own for business purposes. This form can have its advantages and is often used in the beginning stages of a business. Advantages include profits going straight to the owner; no special taxation; it's easy and inexpensive to form; and you have direct control of the business unlike other forms. These may all sound fine and dandy, but the end goal should be asset protection so this form will not suffice for extended periods of time. This is due to several disadvantages that include you being responsible for all debt, which expose you to unlimited liability. This means that if you are sued under this business form you could lose your business as well as personal assets such as your home. Also, it's hard to raise capital and can take up large portions of your time, time that you could use to create more assets (see introduction for time reference).

Partnerships

A partnership is an association that consists of two or more people coming together as co workers for the purpose of owning and operating a business for profit. With this form, much like a sole proprietorship, there's no separation between the owners in regards to debt, profits, or being sued. The partnership form as referenced now is in relationship to general partnerships and limited partnership, not family limited partnership which was previously discussed. I'm talking about taking on outside partners who provide access to equity in return for ownership. In this form of partnership, the general partner would be the person actually running the business and would be the only one facing unlimited liability for any debt whereas the limited partner or partners are only liable up to the amount invested in the business. Partnerships of this kind are easy and inexpensive to form and allows for an unlimited number of partners with no special taxation. The downside to this form is that you'll have to share profits, there's difficulty in transferring ownership, and any possible conflicts that arise can lead to the partnership dissolving. Be careful when deciding to start a business with outside partners or family members whom you aren't transferring assets to.

Corporations

A corporation can be defined as a business entity that legally functions separate and apart from its owners. For legal purposes, a corporation can sue or be sued; sell, purchase, or own property. This structure has many advantages: the owner's liability is limited to the amount invested in the company, much like a limited partnership; the life of the business is not tied to the investors; and ifs easy to raise capital for expansion or other business purposes. A corporation is owned legally by its shareholders or owners who elect a board of directors. They are responsible for appointing management who determine policies and the overall direction of the business. This form can be a good way to protect yourself and your assets but has some drawbacks such as double taxation and some government restrictions. On top of that this form can be costly and complex to form. Many of the drawbacks to a corporation are the reason why LLCs became popular.

We have now reached the end of our journey together, at least for now. Our little journey together is one that I believe will bear fruit for you in the near future. The different ways that were provided within should have sparked your desire to live your best life and find strategic ways to build long-term wealth and boss up. I encourage you to reread each chapter, highlight and take notes, as well as encourage family and friends to grab a copy so that they too can become self-made. Be on the lookout for my upcoming *Money Master Series* and more in-depth books pertaining to financial success. Thank you for spending your time and money with *Self-Made: How to Win by Investing in Yourself.*

WHO IS CARLING D. COLBERT, SR.?

I'm a military veteran and the father to four gifted children. I served my country for eight years that included two combat tours, one to Iraq and the other to Afghanistan. My mission, since 2014, has been to spread financial literacy and give education to the underserved members of society. I was once part of the "rat race" before I went to college for a bachelor's degree in Business and later on taught myself the basics of finance. I can tell you from experience that being financially ignorant hurts, and not just you, but entire generations can be affected.

I got into finance after ending up in military confinement where I hadn't accumulated any assets and was left with thousands of dollars in consumer debt and liabilities. This caused me to reevaluate my life and the previous choices I'd made, which led me to correspondence college courses and investing in every book I could find on the subjects of money, finance, business, and the psychology of wealth. The culmination of my studies created *Self-Made: How to Win by Investing in Yourself* and my upcoming *Money Master Series* that will breakdown each element of my C.I.T.R.A.S. method.

My actions and studies not only led me to write several manuscripts, but to also start finding ways to give back. I decided that a portion of all sales from every book that I'll publish will go to funding a project I call Operation HOT GRITS, which stands for helping our troops get reintegrated to society that will help ex-military felons find living situations. The long-term goal is to have operations in Texas, New York, North Carolina, and Kansas with the home base being in Georgia. The project will look to provide jobs, housing, temporary transportation, and financial education so the recruits can be successful in their communities. There is already a GoFundMe page setup for donations that can be found via Darchelly Pretty on Facebook if you'd like to do more.

Also, a large donation will go to help Autism Speaks as I have several family members with this diagnosis; and to finish it off I intend to make a yearly donation to a charity of my family's choice that will help women and children who have experienced abuse. I can't do anything about the past, but I am looking to effect change and by you purchasing this book, you're helping me make that happen.

I am up for receiving any fan mail, questions, concerns, or criticism you may have about me or any publications I have written thus far. As of now, you can contact me at the address below:

My name
1300 N Warehouse Rd
Ft Leavenworth KS 66027-2304

If my address should change, I will gladly let you know. Thank you all and may The Great Architect of the Universe bless you all.